THE 12 VOLT DOCTOR'S TROUBLESHOOTING BOOK

by Edgar J. Beyn

8-93

Published by: C. PLATH NORTH AMERICAN DIVISION
                  222 Severn Avenue
                  Annapolis, MD U.S.A. 21403

ISBN 1-878797-03-4

Introduction

Imagine having tools in hand, meters, solder, wire, lamps, instructions, spares, wiring diagram all standing by, ready to make a repair. None will do any good at all unless you know where to make the repair: you have to do troubleshooting to locate the cause of a problem. And then you can repair it.

This book is intended to help you search, with tests which are usually very simple. The repairs often are simple, too. That leaves the task of applying the right test at the right place, to identify a problem as directly as possible and avoiding tests at other places which may be frustrating, time consuming, and with a lower probability of success. We want to look at a large number of possible tests and discuss why often just one or two of them are most likely to pinpoint a trouble spot.

Even though boats have become so elaborately fitted with electrical and electronic equipment, problems usually come one at a time, your troubleshooting can focus on just one circuit or one piece of equipment at a time, as with a cabin lights problem, alternator problem, or an engine instruments problem. You will see how to use a simple sketch of just that one circuit, and never mind any over all wiring diagram which probably is so perfectly complete as to make it unattractive for our purposes.

You might also like this ultimate goal, gaining a greater degree of self sufficiency, by trying this book when next there is some electrical trouble, becoming familiar with the tools and test equipment and, most of all, getting to better know your boat.

Your comments and questions are invited, as are your suggestions toward making the book more complete or more useful.

Edgar J. Beyn
BEYN & EPPENDORF
616 Third St.
Annapolis MD 21403
Phone 301 267-0319
Fax 301 267-0452
January 1990

i

ALL TESTS ASSUME
THAT
1. BOAT HAS NEG. GROUND
2. BOAT HAS
   BATT.⊖ CONNECTED
   TO ENGINE BLOCK
(THAT IS, BOAT DOES NOT
HAVE ISOLATED MINUS : ONLY
USED ON ~~ITS~~ SOME METAL HULLS).

Table of Contents

CIRCUIT SKETCH

You are at a serious disadvantage when you look at the wires in **SKETCH 1** and try to figure out what it is supposed to do. Because at one time, someone made the wire connections with schematic in hand, and made a perfectly clear plan on paper into tangles of wires. When you face trouble shooting on such detail, it is almost always worth while to first make a wiring sketch, schematic, or wiring diagram of just that part of the boat's wiring which you are investigating.

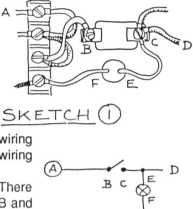

You start by looking at the components. There is the back of a switch with two terminals, B and C. With only two terminals, it must be a single pole switch. Then there is the back of a lamp socket with wire leads E and F. Since a lamp will only light if it is somehow connected to plus and minus, the terminals on the terminal strip are likely plus at top, and minus at the bottom. You verify that with your voltmeter or test light and then make your sketch.

SKETCH 2 simplifies what you actually see. It leaves out the curves and interconnecting jumper wires on the terminal strip, and it ignores that there are wires which are leaving the terminal strip and the switch to places unknown. It just shows that there is a plus terminal A, connected to the switch terminals B and C, feeding both the lamp (a pilot light?) and wire D and another unknown wire. The Lamp is connected at the downstream side of the switch, and has its F leg connected to ground.

This sketch is simple and clear enough to let you decide whether such circuit makes sense. From the purpose of your trouble shooting expedition you will be able to decide that a switch which turns some equipment on, and at the same time lights a lamp makes sense. That then makes your circuit sketch become your most important tool, and the planning and record keeping device for the trouble shooting.

In this example, you would obviously test the connections between A and B which, in the circuit sketch, are just a single conductor. You might eventually find out where the unmarked wire on which terminal C goes, and then, if necessary, expand the circuit sketch. But for your first approach, a simple sketch will show you best what absolutely has to be, to make the equipment on wire D work, and you can then select your tests.

A color felt pen, or just a different pen lets you mark the sections in the circuit sketch which you have tested and found to be in tact. You could mark A as having plus 12 Volt. C, E, and D having plus 12 Volt when the switch is closed. F being properly grounded. Or you would run into the problem when you find things to be different from what the sketch demands.

EXAMPLE

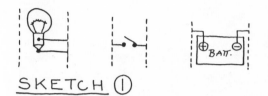

SKETCH ①

Let us start with something simple: a light does not work. **SKETCH 1** shows the light at left, a switch which normally turns the light on and off, and the battery which supplies power.

The sketch also shows what we normally have to live with in boat's wiring: wires between the light and its switch, and between switch and battery can not be traced, run behind bulkheads, in conduits or harnesses, are not numbered or color coded, and are only visible directly at the light and switch. That is normal, and we can do with it.

You will have tried these first steps before thinking about serious and systematic trouble shooting:

1. switched on other lights to test that battery is charged, battery main switch is on,

2. checked that circuit breaker for the light is on,

3. checked or replaced the lamp ("light bulb").

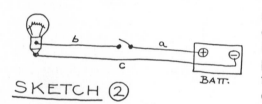

SKETCH ②

As a first step in trouble shooting, make a sketch of the complete circuit for the light, as in **SKETCH 2**. There are several possible problems, some of them are much more likely than others: it is very unlikely that the wires "a" or "b" have broken and separated. It is just as unlikely that the minus wire "c" has broken. However, we usually have the switches in the plus wires, and unswitched minus wires gathering other minus wires on the way to engine ground and on, to battery minus. We therefore have to be suspicious of joints in the minus wire "c". Most likely trouble spots are at the ends of wires, directly at the light and switch, and at the contacts between lamp and lamp socket, and much lower on the list of likely problem spots, the contacts in the switch.

SKETCH 3 shows just three tests which you carry out with a test light or voltmeter.

TEST 1 tells if power gets to the light. It tests through all plus wires and battery main switch, circuit breaker, and light switch, and all minus wiring. Since you already checked or switched the light bulb, you more or less already did this test and,

SKETCH ③

by moving the bulb, rubbed the contacts in the socket, to possibly scrape any corrosion off.

TEST 2 checks two things at once: it tells if there is power out of the switch, and it checks that without depending on the minus wire. If there is no voltage or test light stays dark, trouble is in the switch or, less likely, in circuit breaker or plus wire to the switch. But if there is voltage, or test light is bright, trouble is in the minus wire, between light minus terminal and battery minus: likely nearer the light at some junction, rather than near engine ground since other equipment on the boat is working which also depends on a connection to minus/ground.

TEST 3 tests the switch itself. With the switch closed as sketched, voltage or a bright test light would tell of a faulty switch which is not conducting.

GOAL

The circuit in **SKETCH 4** could be any one, light, motor, or electronic component, while all switches are turned on. Everything as then conducting with the only exception of the break, the problem spot which keeps the equipment from working.

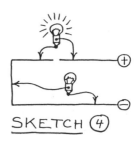

The two test lights demonstrate our trouble shooting goal: we want the test to tell us where the trouble is. It will do that with the greatest precision if we can place the test light wires as closely as possible, just upstream and downstream of the trouble spot.

The circuit in **SKETCH 4** is not very realistic and might rather look like the one in **SKETCH 5**. But the goal is the same. A poor connection of a wire to the equipment switch SW has caused trouble. **TEST 1** tells that power does not reach the equipment terminals. **TEST 2** would tell that the problem is somewhere between battery main switch and EQ., **TEST 3** narrows down the trouble area to the location of switch SW, and **TEST 4** finally points out the bad connection between wire and switch terminal. Once that has been found, the repair is easy.

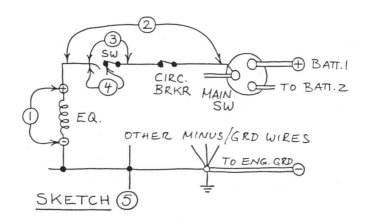

TOOLS

Voltage measurements are probably most important in our electrical trouble shooting. There are several choices among the useful tools, with some advantages and serious disadvantages. Most important: a more expensive voltmeter or one with higher accuracy will only very rarely do a better job. In fact, sometimes a test light, consisting of a light bulb with test wires, will give more useful information about the presence or absence of voltage than a very sensitive and expensive digital voltmeter. The reason is shown in **SKETCH 1**. There is a badly corroded switch contact. The switch is connected to plus 12 Volt on one side. You are measuring between its other side and ground, for example as

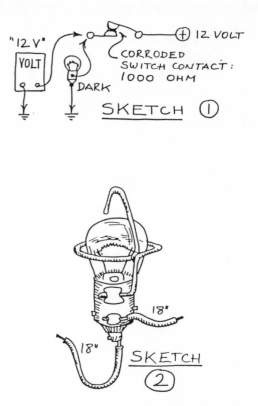

a check before connecting some equipment. Even though there are 1000 Ohms of resistance between switch contacts, the digital voltmeter and other voltmeters with high internal resistance and high sensitivity will announce 12 Volt, and not alert you to the corroded contacts. But a test light with 12 Volt lamp will remain dark, as would any cabin light which you might have connected to the faulty switch.

The explanation is that the test light will draw up to one half Ampere to light up, and will not light if not enough current can flow. The sensitive meter, on the other hand, will produce a reading with only a minute current, and 1000 Ohms of resistance on the way to the meter just do not matter. But such high sensitivity in our applications can lead to errors: you may detect voltages which reach the meter through your body, just because you may touch 12 Volt, or hold the ends of wires together with one end.

For this reason, avoid the temptation to buy a more expensive meter because you hope that it might find the trouble faster. Fine if it is more rugged, but it does not come with a brain.

SKETCH 2 shows how to make a test light. Start with a 12 Volt lamp as used in car tail lights or small cabin lights, best with single contact bayounet base and 2 to 5 Watt. Use very flexible stranded wire and solder the ends directly to the lamp base as shown. Connect an alligator clip to each test wire.

Solder a length of solid copper wire to the lamp base and bend it into a lamp guard and hook. Make the wires about 18 inches long.

You likely have a Volt Ohm Meter (VOM) or pocket meter on the boat which will serve for the purpose. If not, look at the least expensive VOM at your local electronics store: there is one for just over ten dollars which has a 0–15 Volt DC range, perfect for the 12 Volt system since it makes use of almost the full scale length for 12 Volt (11 to 14 Volt) battery systems, much better that the usual 0–10 Volt and 0–50 Volt ranges which are too small, or too large for good resolution. That little meter is by far my favorite.

A digital Voltmeter has two important applications, in spite of our earlier discussion. First of all, it can measure very low resistances which to an analog VOM will all look like zero Ohm, and its high resolution of Volt measurements can be used to measure voltage drop through wiring when the size of the current is known, or to calculate current when the length and wire gauge of a wire is known, applications which are described in a later section.

We have already come across tests with light or meter where a measurement is made between battery main switch and, for example, a cabin light switch. That is a distance impossible to reach with the wires on all meters. Since long wires on test lights and voltmeters tend to be a nuisance when you have to untangle them and then wrap them up again, a few very long extension test wires are useful. Make them from No. 16 or 14 stranded wire and solder alligator clips to each end. Have one long enough to reach from battery compartment to the farthest place below deck, and possibly one to reach the mast top. These wires will then also be long enough to make measurements between engine ground and dock ground at outlets on shore, in corrosion trouble shooting.

Finally, a small scouting pocket compass, or the boat's hand bearing compass, is a handy tool to detect currents in electrical wires. How to do that is described in a separate section. Try if your hand bearing compass will do. Otherwise find a Boy Scout's compass with very mobile, undampened needle and make it a part of your trouble shooting tools. How the compass detects direct current is discussed in the next section.

Volt Ohm Meters (VOM)

Occasionally, there may be trouble with the VOM, your most important tool. If you have touched it to voltage while it was switched to measure Ohms, an internal fuse or fure wire or jumper may have burned out. Open the meter case and look for a fure which is rare in small VOMs, or look for a very thin wire, usually nickel or tin plated, which had connected two pads on the printed circuit board, as shown in **SKETCH 1**. Replace such fuse wire by first unsoldering the old wire ends. Then connect a new fuse jumper wire as in the sketch, use a single strand from a thin and very flexible piece of stranded wire. You will be able to judge if your replacement wire is about right by comparing with the left overs of the old one.

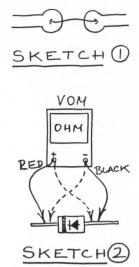

The Ohm meter part has an internal battery. Test the battery by switching to the lowest Ohm range, then touch red and black test leads to each other. The meter should read zero Ohm, or you should be able to adjust it to show zero Ohm by the adjustment control. A low battery will not let you adjust to zero. Weak batteries may change their supply voltage while you make Ohm measurements and will then cause false readings.

While you replace the battery, note that many VOMs have the plus battery terminal connected to the red meter lead, something which is immaterial for Ohm measurements but is important when testing diodes. If you cannot see the battery connections inside, and there is no other VOM handy to test yours, us a small diode and test as in **SKETCH 2**. Meter is switched to Ohm, lowest range if there are choices. Note the band or stripe on the diode which marks the cathode or minus terminal. In the sketch, the meter would show infinite Ohms (meter needle not moving) if battery is internally connected with plus on plus/red meter wire, wires touched to diode as by solid lines.

It is likely that the internal battery has its plus pole on the black meter wire. Meter then shows about 1 k Ohm when connected as the solid lines, and infinite Ohms when reversed as with dashed lines. Bets, keep a diode in your electrical box as a reference when testing diodes. Useful types, available in radio and electronics stores or from a TV repair shop are 1N4000, 1N4001, 1N4003, 1N4004; or 1N5400, 1N5401, and higher end digits, value under a quarter.

Digital VOMs on the other hand, usually have the internal battery plus pole on the red meter wire. These meters have a diode testing range which gives the forward voltage drop of the diode in Volts (silicon diodes 0.3 to 0.8 V) and give no reading when leads are reversed. These meters may not give any readings with diodes on their Ohm ranges, so the diode setting, marked with a diode symbol as that in **SKETCH 2**, must be used.

SAME PROBLEM SPOTTED
BY DIFFERENT TESTS

We are now working our way toward the proper choice of tests. **SKETCHES 1 and 2** show a circuit consisting of plus and minus wires and a "load" which is some electrical equipment. There is one fault: a gap in the plus wire which could be a faulty switch contact, loose connection at a terminal, blown fuse, or loose crimp. Except for this interruption in the plus wiring, all switches are closed, meaning that they are turned on, making contact, so that ordinarily, current would flow through the load.

The fault could be detected in two different ways: if a voltmeter were connected to bridge the gap, as at the top of **SKETCH 1**, it would show 12 Volt (actually, the exact voltage of the battery which may be slightly higher or lower). With a test light, as in **SKETCH 2**, the light would become bright if connected across the gap, as at the top of that sketch.

The fault could also be spotted by two other tests which are shown in both sketches: measuring the voltage present just before the gap or fault, and its absence just downstream would point out the fault. With the test light, a bright light just before the gap, and a dark light just downstream as in **SKETCH 2** would tell that there is a break which prevents plus 12 Volt from reaching the light at the right.

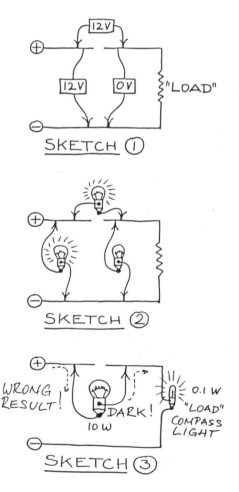

In practice, both methods are commonly used, depending on ease of access. There are several examples in the following sections which use one or the other method. Comparing with the earlier example, the dark light at right in **SKETCH 2** is the same test as the test light test 1 in **SKETCH 3** in the EXAMPLE, except that the test location here more closely locates the spot of the break.

You should understand one important detail: the test at the top of the sketches here, with voltmeter or test light bridging the fault or break, depends on the electrical equipment or load to be switched on, and the wiring between load and ground to be in tact, because the minus wire of the voltmeter, or the minus or "downstream" wire of the test light depend on the conductivity through load and minus wire to the battery minus terminal, in order to show a voltage or to light up.

Almost all electrical equipment including running lights, cabin lights, blowers, other motors, electronic gear, would provide this connection to ground for any voltmeter and would have internal resistances low enough to make a typical test light become bright. However, a very powerful test light with, say, a 10

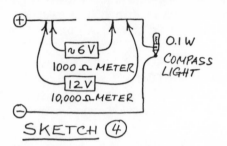

SKETCH ④

Watt lamp, used to test a load which happens to be a very small and dim compass light of, for example, 0.1 Watt, would then be connected as in **SKETCH 3**: the compass light "load" would not allow enough current to flow to brighten the test light. To calculate the details, find the current for the test light, then the current for the compass light, and compare the two: the compass light is the bottle neck which limits current for the two lights in series.

In comparison, a very simple, inexpensive VOM or voltmeter may have about 1000 Ohm internal resistance meaning that, connected to 12 Volt, it will draw a current of 0.012 Ampere, which makes it have 0.144 Watt, similar in size to this very small compass light load. In place of the test light, this meter would show a voltage when connected at one side of the fault in **SKETCH 3**, and zero Volt at the other, as in **SKETCH 4**.

Better voltmeters, with higher internal resistance, would give readings close to the full battery voltage, no matter how small the load or how high the load resistance, up to the point where meter sensitivity can play tricks, as mentioned earlier in the section on tools.

Compass Detects Current

It is often impractical to space an ammeter into a wire, to find out if a current is flowing in the wire. Sometimes, it is outright dangerous to do that: the unknown current may be greater than the ammeter can handle, causing the meter to go up in smoke. Or it can destroy voltage regulators if an ammeter were connected at an alternator's output terminal and during the test, ammeter wires should come loose.

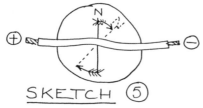

SKETCH (5)

Currents from about ½ Ampere up can be found with a compass. A small hand bearing compass or boy scout compass works well. As in **SKETCH 5**, have the wire which you are investigating run across the face of the compass, from East to West, not from North to South. Now switch the battery or power on and off. If there is a (direct) current flowing, the compass card or needle will swing as indicated in the sketch.

The compass card will swing in the opposite direction if

1. current flows in the opposite direction. That is, plus and minus are reversed,

2. the wire runs under the compass, instead of over, as sketched.

Only direct current works, and only a single wire should be tested at a time. Two wires in a cable, or twisted together, and carrying current in one wire to some equipment, and the same current back in the other wire will cancel each other's magnetic field and will therefore not affect the compass. And wires running North to South over the compass will either increase or decrease the earth magnetic lines but not change their direction and, therefore, also not cause the compass card to swing.

The magnetic field generated by direct current in a wire is used by ammeters which can be clamped on to a wire, over the insulation, and without any electrical connections. Such meters are useful when you have to measure starter current, or other high currents. Such meters for lower DC current ranges require that the wire be wrapped several turns around a part of the meter body, to generate sufficient magnetism, as the meter by Faria Corp., Uncasville, CT., in **SKETCH 6**. As a trouble shooting tool, its use is restricted by the needed length of extra wire which often is not available.

Most often, we determine indirectly that there must be a current flowing if a voltage is present, and if a conductive path is available, as determined by Ohm measurements.

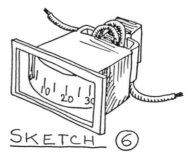

SKETCH (6)

The Electric Starter

Engine starter motors draw substantial currents from their battery and can develop sizeable power for very short lengths of time. Most often, their wiring is as in **SKETCH 1**.

The motor consists of the armature and commutator which turn, and the housing with field coils. Both the armature and field coils are made from thick wire or flat copper bands. The field coils with their iron cores are tightly crowded around the space for the armature, such that for some, special tools and fixtures are used to get the assembled: it is not practical to disassemble the larger starter motors on board.

Current reaches the starter from the battery by the starter "cables", usually from battery plus posts to battery selector switch, to the plus terminal on the starter solenoid, a heavy relay which normally sits directly on top of the starter motor. The starter solenoid switches starting current on when its coil, see **SKETCH 1**, is connected to battery voltage. With smaller engines, current to the starter solenoid comes directly from the engine key switch or engine starter button. With engines over 30 HP or so, the starter solenoid coil draws enough current to require another relay and the arrangement in the sketch.

Let SW1 be the engine key switch and SW2 the starter button. With the battery main switch on, battery power reaches the plus terminal of the starter solenoid and the key switch. Closing (that is, turning on) the key switch and pressing (closing) the starter button SW2 lets current flow through the relay coil and close the relay contact. The relay contacts can carry the higher current (for example, 10 Amps) needed by the starter solenoid coil. Current continues to ground and back to the battery minus post.

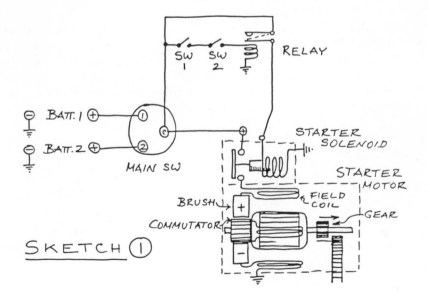

SKETCH 1

The electromagnet in the solenoid pulls a copper disc with sudden force against heavy copper posts, to connect power to the starter motor. The sketch shows the motor current going through field coil, then by brushes through the armature coils, then through an other field coil, to ground. That may not be true for your starter which may have field and armature in parallel. For our trouble shooting, that detail is not important.

On the motor shaft in **SKETCH 1** is the small gear which is engaged in the teeth of the engine flywheel just before or during the first turn of the starter motor. In some starters, the gear slides along steep rifle grooves on the shaft so that the first turns of the motor make the small gear move sideways before its mass can get accelerated to turn. The side motion engages the gears. In other designs, the solenoid electromagnet has two jobs: with an arm, it shifts the starter gear to mesh with flywheel teeth and, as it moves further, closes the electrical contact for starter current.

Trouble with engine starting could be due to non-electrical causes which are not covered in this book. Electrical causes could be:

1. Battery problems

2. Wiring problems in the heavy battery and starter "cables"

3. Contact problems in solenoid or starter motor

4. Problems in switches, relays, and their wiring, electrical engine equipment such as safety arrangements such as start-in-neutral switches, don't-start-while-engine-running systems.

Trouble Shooting:

1. *Battery problems*

The high current drawn by starter motors will almost certainly affect the voltage of the starter battery. Test, by watching a cabin light powered by the same battery as the engine, or connect a test light or voltmeter to that battery. The

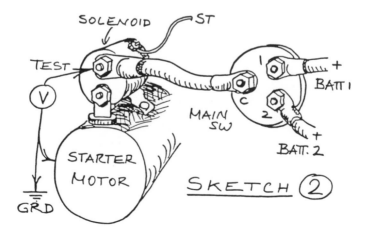

starter motor draws current, and the starter solenoid makes contact, if you hear the usual loud click of the solenoid when you push the start button and the light dims, or the voltmeter reading falls from above 12 Volt to 10 Volt or below, regardless whether the starter motor actually cranks.

If the voltmeter falls below 9 Volt, or cabin light or test light dim to orange-brown color, the battery is the cause of trouble. Recharge, or switch batteries, or connect another battery in parallel.

If the starter button or key switch produce the usual loud click of the starter solenoid but the cabin light does not dim, or the voltmeter shows only a slight drop in voltage, and the starter motor does not crank the engine, test with the voltmeter or test light if battery power reaches the solenoid. See **SKETCH 2**.

If you don't find plus voltage at the solenoid plus terminal, be suspicious of the meter or test light ground connection. Test at another ground spot on the engine, some clean, unpainted metal area. If indeed there is no plus 12 Volt, or whatever voltage your system has, at the solenoid, see the next places upstream: the terminals at the battery main switch. An again, think about the battery minus connections: they must be as sound and solid as the plus wires or the starter will not work. If your trouble is here, the cure should be straight forward.

2. *Connections*

Should you measure the proper voltages but the starter still will not turn, or draws heavy current but will not produce enough power to turn the engine, even though the batteries are in good shape, make a test for poor connections in the battery "cables" and terminals. A connection with only a small fraction of an Ohm in resistance, perfectly suitable for all other equipment on the boat including the anchor windlass, may be too resistive for the starter.

EXAMPLE:

A starter motor with a resistance of 0. 05 Ohm is connected with a bad terminal, with 0.05 Ohm. All other wires are perfect and have no resistance at all. The battery is big and supplies 12 Volt at all times. Compared to perfect wires, the bad terminal causes a 6 Volt drop, see **SKETCH 3**. That leaves only 6 Volt at the starter. The current is only half of the current with perfect wires because there is now double the resistance. With only half the current through the starter, at only half the voltage, the starter will only develop one quarter of the watts, or one quarter of the power compared with perfect wiring. Because the

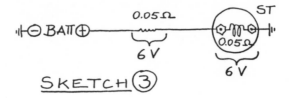

starter Watts are calculated by multiplying Amps (now half of perfect) with Volts (now only half of perfect).

Test starter wiring for resistive connections: with batteries switched on, starter motor drawing heavy current, push the starter button and hold down for 5 to 10 seconds or longer. If the engine should turn or start, keep ignition off or pull kill lever at the same time, to keep the starter motor working for 5 to 10 seconds. Turn power off, have engine off, and feel all battery posts, terminals, main switch posts, lugs on battery cables, starter solenoid terminals, ground strap and terminals, grounding bolts, minus cables to batteries. Feel for warm places which indicate resistance, from heat generated with the starter current flowing.

3. Switch Contacts

Bad contacts inside battery main switches can be improved by having all electrical equipment on board switched off, then switching the battery main switch back and forth through all of its four positions ten or twenty times, or as long as you can stand it. The mechanical action between the copper contacts will rub the surfaces clean where it counts, best if all possible arcing is prevented by having no current drawn on the boat.

Starter solenoid contact trouble is likely if the batteries are in good shape, the battery and starter "cables" with all of their lugs and terminals and the ground strap and minus connections have been tested, and the starter solenoid clicks as usual, but the starter motor does not crank.

SKETCH 4 shows how you can exercise and mechanically recondition the contacts in the solenoid switch. Turn the battery main switch OFF so that all electrical equipment on the boat is without power. Prepare a sufficiently long wire of size 12 and connect one end to plus 12 Volt, for example at the battery terminals of the main switch, or directly at a plus battery post, while securing the other end of the wire. Then take the other end of the wire to the starter solenoid and touch the small terminal on the solenoid which normally brings power from the start button, see the sketch.

As you touch that terminal with the wire, you will experience sparks and arcing normal for about 10 Ampere, and the solenoid will pull in with its usual

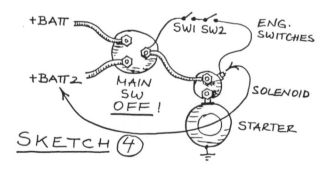

SKETCH ④

powerful click. But the starter motor will not turn because all other power is turned off.

The solenoid electromagnet is powerful: it pulls a copper disk on to two copper posts with the speed of a closing mouse trap, with the impact of a hammer blow. Since there now is no current flowing, and arcing completely eliminated, the action between copper disk and contacts will now be able to smooth out old pit marks, clear away oxide caused by arcing, and expose clean contact surfaces.

A design feature of most solenoid switches is that the copper disk is free to rotate, so that from time to time, new places at its edges make the contact between the fixed copper posts. In our case, that may be a disadvantage because the newly cleared spots on the disk may turn away with use, and you then may have to go through the procedure again. After having bad solenoid contact trouble for the first time, keep the long wire in the engine room, in case the engine must be started urgently while the solenoid gives trouble again. Then make a permanent repair when circumstances allow.

By the way, the small terminal on the starter solenoid is the same to which you would jump power, to start the engine when key switch, start button, relays, or their wiring do not work, or the key has been lost. To start the engine in that way, power would be switched on, and the big starter solenoid terminal with battery "cable" would be at plus 12 Volt. A screwdriver is usually enough to bridge between this big plus terminal and the smaller coil plus terminal, to start the engine.

4. Problems in relays, switches, and their wiring

We are now looking at the relatively thin wires and components between the start button or key switch and the starter solenoid. In the simplest case, as on smaller engines, there will be just a single wire from start button directly to the small coil terminal of the starter solenoid. The wire then connects plus 12 Volt from key switch or button to the coil, to have the solenoid coil switch on starter motor current.

More often, there is a relay involved, as in **SKETCH 1**, because often, more current is needed by the starter solenoid than a key switch can handle. In that sketch, the switches must supply only about 1 Ampere to the relay coil. The relay contacts are chosen to deal with up to 10 Amps, or more in large starters, the current drawn by the starter solenoid. The wiring of such single relay already offers some options which make the trouble shooting more difficult, see **SKETCH 5**.

The switch may be key switch with start contact, or the start button, or take it as meaning both of

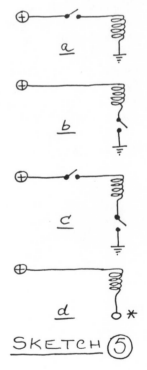

SKETCH ⑤

them. Really devious wiring could have these two on different sides of the relay coil. That coil is shown in all four examples in **SKETCH 5**.

The switch at a is on the plus side of the coil, same as in **SKETCH 1**. The other side of the coil is shown connected to ground. Closing the switch would power the relay coil.

The switch could also be in the minus wire, as shown at b. With more elaborate engine wiring, there often are other switches which control starting, as with the additional switch at c. One switch would be the start button or key switch with start contact, the other may be a switch at the gear shift, the switch closed only when in neutral, and open when in forward or reverse, and then preventing starting. That extra switch could also be an oil pressure or fuel pressure switch, normally closed, but open when the engine is running, thus preventing that the starter be engaged accidentally while the engine is running.

Finally, at d, the minus wire of the relay coil ends at a terminal which is the excite or D+ terminal of an alternator: a terminal which is able to take the relay coil current and allow it to flow to ground while the alternator is not running, with the engine stopped. This alternator terminal, **SKETCH 6**, rises to plus 12 Volt when the alternator is running, so that, with the engine running, relay current no longer can flow to ground. Pushing the start button with the engine running would then have no effect: the button would only apply 12 Volt to one side of the relay coil while there already is 12 Volt at the other end. The relay would not work. This is another arrangement to prevent starting while the engine already runs. Additional details are in the section on alternator trouble shooting. This wiring method is used on some Perkins engines and probably others.

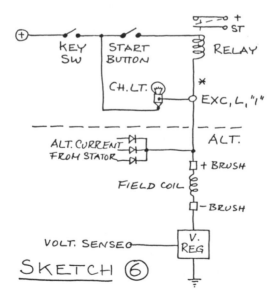

SKETCH ⑥

Alternator

The alternator has two functions on the boat. It is designed for one of them, and excels. It must do the other, but often fits that function badly. The first is to supply all electrical power needed by electrical equipment while the engine runs. This is the job alternators do very well on cars, so that low or high currents can be drawn for unlimited time, without affecting the battery.

The other function is of great importance especially on sail boats: the alternator must recharge the batteries after current has been drawn from batteries while the alternator was off. Its design places the emphasis on high current output when suddenly high current is demanded by equipment, while at other times gently recharging a battery without overcharging it. Understanding the alternator's performance will help you judge whether there is trouble with the alternator, or whether it performs as designed, though perhaps badly for the application.

Alternators work closely with their voltage regulator which often is inside the alternator, sometimes attached to the alternator, or more rarely a separate, external component. The performance of the alternator can be checked without tools, by observation:

Watch a cabin light before and after you start the engine. Its brightness and color will usually change to greater brightness and from yellowish to more nearly white color when the alternator begins to charge and battery voltage rises. This will tell you that the alternator is charging, but will not tell anything about voltage regulator or actual charging current.

With any alternator trouble, it will help greatly to know the make and some details of your alternator. The following list tells which alternators were fitted as original equipment on brands of marine engines. The listing also tells if voltage regulators are internal, attached, or external, and if the alternator design is type P or N, something discussed later. If you have another unidentifiable alternator, look at its back and note appearance and terminals, see **SKETCH 1**.

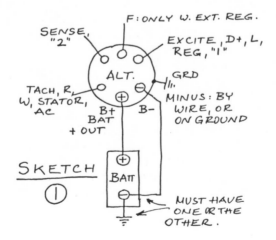

Engine brand	Alternator	Volt. Reg.	Type
Caterpillar	Motorola	attached	P
Ford Lehman	Motorola	attached	P
Ford, British	CAV, Lucas	internal	N
GM Detroit	Delco	internal	N
Perkins, US	Delco	internal	N
Perkins, Brit.	CAV, Lucas	internal	N
Universal	Motorola	various	P
Volvo, older	SEV Marchal	attached	P
Volvo, recent	Paris-Rhone	internal	N
Westerbeke, older	Motorola	attached	p
Westerbeke, recent	Mitsubishi	internal	N
Yanmar	Hitachi	internal	N

Tachometer, stator, TACH, R, W, connected internally to the stator alternating current, has wire connected to tachometer (tachometer signal). Easily added, it may be a wire outof a vent hole in the housing, instead of terminal.

The connections to the battery in **SKETCH 1** will often include an Ampere meter between B+ and battery plus, and may have a battery selector switch, discussed in the section on batteries. The minus wire will be as shown if the alternator has an isolated minus terminal, or will in part be replaced by alternator bracket and engine block.

Alternator has no output

Visible on the ammeter which shows no needle motion after engine has been started and brought to higher RPM, and verified by voltmeter: meter reading before the engine is started shows battery voltage, typically between 11.5 and 12.5 Volt. After the engine has been started, this voltage remains same or decreases slightly. If there is a charge light on the engine panel, charge light becomes bright when key switch or engine circuit breaker are turned on, and light remains bright after the engine has picked up speed.

SKETCH 1 shows possible terminals of the alternator, usually at the back, or on the back housing which is the end of the alternator opposite of the pulley.

Your alternator will have some of the terminal and may have some others. The terminals and their purpose are:

Plus output terminal, B+, BAT, has heavy wire connected to battery plus post, or to battery selector switch "common" terminal, or to starter solenoid plus terminal, or to an ammeter which then has its other wire connected to those places.

Minus terminal, B-, GRD, MINUS, is either connected inside alternator to alternator housing and then conducts through alternator bracket to engine block, through engine ground wire to battery minus bost, or is separate minus output terminal: this terminal must then be connected by heavy wire, same as plus output wire, to battery minus.

Excite terminal, EXC, D+, L, REG, "1" (number 1), on almost all alternators except few "self exciting", its wiring shown in **SKETCH 2**. This terminal is usually connected to the charge light on engine panel.

Field terminal, F, F1, F2, indicates that the alternator has an external voltage regulator, connected with a wire to the field terminal. Has become rare.

Sense terminal, S, SENSE, "2" (number 2), is a terminal of the internal voltage regulator and is connected to battery plus pole, indirectly by wire to key switch or engine circuit breaker. On many alternators, connected inside alternator to plus output terminal.

SKETCH 2 shows the wiring of a charge or idiot light. With the light becoming bright, some excite current is likely reaching the alternator. Test if excite current is too low:

1. Increase engine speed, to see whether charge light then goes out, or

2. use a test light or a jumper wire and connect the excite terminal through the test light, or directly, to plus 12 Volt. Then restart the engine, note if ammeter now shows alternator output, or if an increase in battery voltage indicates that the alternator now has output and is charging the battery. The charge light will remain dark when bypassed with the jumper wire.

To increase excite current and to make the alternator "cut in" at lower RPM, replace the charge light bulb with a lamp of greater Watt rating but equal base, or connect another lamp of same wattage, or a power resistor, parallel to the present charge light, as shown in **SKETCH 3**. Use a power resistor of 50 Ohm, 10 Watt which will get warm while the charge light is bright only. Or solder wire leads to another lamp ("light bulb"), and connect it instead of the resistor.

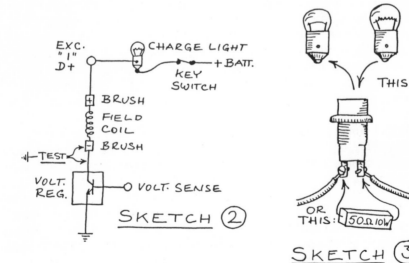

Alternator has no output, excite current OK

Use of the test hole: first make certain what you should have checked before: that the alternator is solidly connected to a battery. You can make a quick check by touching your test light or voltmeter to the B+ and minus terminal or case of the alternator. Then note the small D shaped but unmarked hole on the back of Delco alternators, or the small pin hole or oval hole on many other alternators with internal voltage regulators. A metal pin inserted into these holes will contact a metal tab in Delcos, or the minus brush directly in other alternators of type N with internal regulators. With the pin also touching the alternator housing, the alternator will normally produce full output current since the pin allows full field current to flow: the pin makes a bypass connection to the voltage regulator. See the TEST indicated in **SKETCH 2**.

With output current, the test tells of a faulty voltage regulator while the test without alternator output points to trouble with rectifier diodes or stator windings inside the alternator.

Alternator OK, voltage regulator trouble

In order to deal effectively with voltage regulators, note the two different designs in **SKETCH 4**. The voltage regulator in all alternators controls or throttles field current by being connected in series with the field coil, the coil on the rotor in the alternator which makes the rotor more or less magnetic, so that the alternator produces more or less output power at a given speed. The regulator can do its controlling whether upstream or downstream of the field coil. In "The 12 Volt Doctor's Alternator Book" we have started to call the design on the left type N, the regulator is on the minus or Negative side of the field coil. The other is type P, with the regulator on the Plus or Positive side of field. One works as well as the other, but the regulators are not interchangeable, and trouble shooting is different.

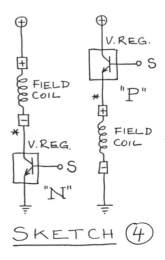

Normal Voltage Regulator Performance

Test battery voltage before and during the first 20 minutes, or up to one hour after engine starting. Test the battery which is being charged by the alternator. Use only one battery for this test since it will make the test shorter. See **SKETCH 5** which shows battery voltage versus time. The sketch gives an example. Your values may be different. Important is only that battery voltage begins to climb when the alternator begins to charge. Voltage continues to climb until battery voltage, that is the same voltage as at the voltage regulator sense terminal, reaches the voltage setting of the voltage regulator. Battery voltage will not rise above this setting. Instead, the voltage regulator will now reduce the so called field current so that the set voltage is being maintained.

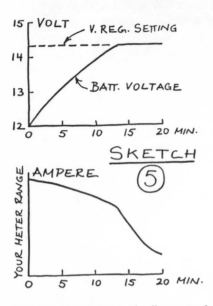

In the lower part of **SKETCH 5** is the corresponding sketch of alternator output current versus time. Until the voltage regulator setting is reached, the alternator works at its maximum output which depends on alternator size and speed, and size and condition of the battery. During this phase, with constant speed, alternator output Amperes drop gradually as battery voltage is being built up. When the regulator voltage, upper sketch, has been reached, Ampere readings decrease more dramatically as the voltage regulator reduces field current, to maintain output voltage.

Your alternator should perform similarly with a functional voltage regulator but voltage regulator setting and minutes needed to reach that setting may vary. Regulator settings typically range from about 14.0 Volt to 14.5 Volt.

Test the response of the voltage regulator to load current: with an ammeter available, switch all cabin lights on after your voltmeter shows that battery voltage has teached the regulator setting and remains constant. With cabin lights now switched on, the ammeter reading should increase by about the amount drawn by the cabin lights. Ammeter reading can increase to the original maximum at the beginning of the engine run. Switch cabin lights, or any other suitable load, off and note that the ammeter reading is falling back.

Caution: see the section on engine instruments. Some engine panel ammeters are wired to show battery charging current only, not total alternator output current, and will then not respond to the voltage regulator load test.

Test the voltage regulator separately

The voltage regulator is more likely to fail than the components of the alternator, such as rectifying diodes or stator windings. But since diodes and windings are relatively easy to check, see those tests and decide whether the regulator must be tested at this stage.

External regulators are easiest to test because they are already accessible. Attached regulators on Motorola, SEV-Marchal, Bosch, and some CAV and Lucas alternators are easily disconnected and tested. Voltage regulators inside Delco alternators are accessible by opening the alternator: all steps can be carried out with hand tools and a small socket set. Internal regulators in Hitachi and Mitsubishi alternators are very difficult to access, remove, or replace and this step is best avoided. Regulators on Paris-Rhone alternators are easy to remove but space for wires is crowded, a nuisance when reconnecting it.

The TEST is best carried out with a small battery and a battery charger which is capable of overcharging the battery. The battery is then able to reach most normal voltage regulator settings up to about 14.5 Volt. **SKETCH 6** shows how to connect the regulator and a test light to the battery. The test light takes the place of the field coil and makes the test foolproof.

The sketch shows how to hook up both type N and type P regulators and seems cluttered. But only one setup will apply to you. Note that in all cases, the voltage sensing terminal of the regulator is connected to plus. In the type N part, you may notice again that the regulator is on the negative side of the test light. The light acts as the field coil.

In the type P arrangement at right, the regulator is on the positive side of the light, or inserted in the plus wire. Compare the earlier table and **SKETCH 4**. Connect a voltmeter to the battery.

The test is simple: connect the regulator and test light to the battery. The light should become fully bright, telling us that full field current would flow, because the battery voltage is bound to be below the regulator voltage setting.

Now have the battery charger increase battery voltage. Above about 13.8 Volt the battery will begin to gas, and you should top up cells with distilled water after the test. Watch the voltmeter and note the reading when the test light suddenly goes out. You should repeat the test a few times: disconnect or unplug the battery charger so that battery voltage falls and the light suddenly turns bright. Then charge again until the light turns dark, and note at which voltage that happens.

Should the light remain bright at or above 15 Volt, the regulator is shorted. It would keep the alternator at full output and eventually overcharge the batteries. If the light is dark at any voltage, the regulator (its power transistor) is open and the alternator would have no output. Voltage settings under 14 Volt would give serious trouble with battery charging by alternator, and settings over 14.5 Volt would be like having no regulator at all, having the alternator at maximum output at all times.

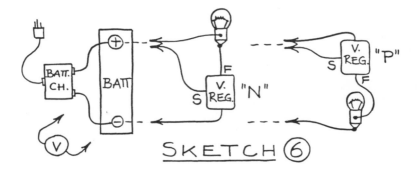

SKETCH 6

Voltage regulator trouble: action

Unless you are in the unusual position of having a spare voltage regulator, some temporary action may be needed to operate the alternator without a faulty regulator. In the case of a shorted regulator, alternator running time, meaning engine running time, may be limited to avoid eventual overcharging of batteries. The alternator MAY NOT be disconnected from the batteries to discontinue charging. Only interruption of field current, or removing the drive belt, can be used to stop output current.

With faulty regulators which are open, make a connection indicated by * in **SKETCH 4**. Connect a test light, or several test lights or 12 Volt lamps in parallel, as follows:

With type N alternators, between minus brush and ground. Make the connection to ground somewhere convenient to disconnect.

With type P alternators, connect test light or lamps between plus brush and plus 12 Volt, such as the alternator plus output terminal, or some place convenient to connect and disconnect.

The current through the test light will flow and bypass the voltage regulator. It is connected in parallel to the faulty voltage regulator, see **SKETCH 4**, and the lest light current will be equal to field current and will produce low alternator output proportional to alternator speed. With additional lamps, more field current will flow and alternator output will be higher. With engine off, lights must be disconnected to avoid draining the battery.

If a voltage regulator of the same type (N or P) but of different make is available, it may be connected by wires to the alternator and will then serve like the original and according to its voltage setting.

With unidentifiable regulators, use the test and **SKETCH 6** to identify type and terminals. Many alternators have other terminals in addition to the necessary field, sense, and plus or minus terminals. Most often, there is also an excite terminal which can be ignored in the test.

Wires on voltage regulators are often color coded with

RED: plus
Black: minus
Green: field
Yellow: excite, or light terminal.

SKETCH 7 shows how to test all diodes with a test light. Note the diode symbol which, in this direction, conducts and makes the lamp light up. In the opposite direction, the diode blocks current. The type of diode shown in the sketch is usually used in alternators. One terminal is its metal housing, the other is the solder terminal which extends from insulating material. This type of diode is made to be press

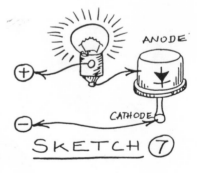

22

fitted into metal "heat sink" holes and is made with metal housing being anode or cathode.

It is unimportant to the test in which sequence the test light and the diode are connected. **SKETCH 8** intends to show you that. It makes no difference if lamp or diode come first. Only the direction of the diode determines whether current flows and the light gets bright. The symbols for lamps ("light bulbs") and diodes are used in this sketch.

We can make a few diode tests from the outside of the alternator. The tests can find some diode problems but not others. See if your alternator has a stator terminal, called TACH (to tachometer), R, or W. Then pick the sketch and tests which apply.

Diode tests for alternators without TACH, R, or W terminal

Test a in **SKETCH 9** has the alternator output wire disconnected but the alternator bracket or minus wire still connected. Touch test light to plus 12 Volt and to the alternator plus output terminal. The lamp should remain dark. If it becomes bright, at least one plus and one minus rectifying diode in the alternator have failed and become shorted. With the light dark, test b is necessary.

Test b in **SKETCH 9** MUST have the alternator isolated from its mounting bracket, or must have the minus wire disconnected from isolated minus terminal. The plus output wire remains disconnected, too.

Connect the alternator plus output wire to ground. Touch the test light to plus 12 Volt and to the alternator housing, or to the alternator minus output terminal if so fitted. The light should become bright, telling that at least one positive and one negative rectifying diode is in tact and working. If the light remains dark, all three minus diodes, or all three plus diodes, or all rectifying diodes in the alternator have failed by becoming open.

If both tests, a and b, give the normal results as in the sketch, the alternator should be able to produce some output. If it did not, further tests must be done at the inside of the alternator, described later.

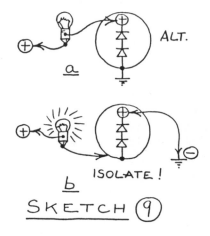

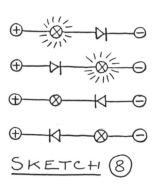

23

Diode tests for alternators with TACH, R, or W terminal

That alternator terminal gives access to the stator windings from the outside, and the plus and minus rectifying diodes can be tested separately. The alternator is shown with minus on housing. Use isolated minus terminal instead if it has that. Resistance of stator windings is so low that only the diodes will affect test results.

Disconnect (and secure) plus output wire. Connect test light as shown in **SKETCH 10**, always one lead to plus 12 Volt. Disconnect alternator from mounting bracket and isolate, for tests c and d. Use another wire to connect to minus or ground as shown.

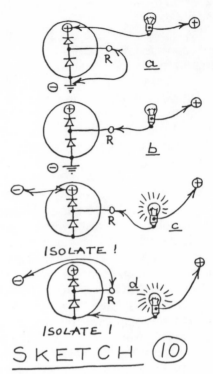

a   light normally dark.
     Bright light: at least
     one positive diode shorted.

b   light normally dark.
     Bright light: at least one negative diode shorted.

c   light normally bright. Dark light: all three positive diodes failed and open.

d   light normally bright. Dark light: all three negative diodes failed and open.

The tests cannot detect one or two positive or negative open diodes, with the remaining diode or diodes in tact. Must use the internal tests.

Testing individual rectifying diodes

SKETCH 11 shows the normal arrangement of three positive diodes and three negative diodes, each on a heat sink or metal plate which then becomes electrically identical to the plus or minus terminal. Each diode has its other terminal connected to the windings of the stator. Since these windings are of relatively heavy solid copper wire, and short, these individual terminals toward the center of the sketch are all connected to each other. For testing with test light or Ohm meter, stator wires must first be unsoldered from each diode. The diode remains a part of its heat sink. Test in two directions, to test conduction and blocking of the diode, as shown in **SKETCH 7** and **SKETCH 8**.

Stator winding test

With a stator terminal such as TACH, R, or W, use Ohm meter between stator terminal and alternator housing. Low Ohm readings, under 1000 Ohm,

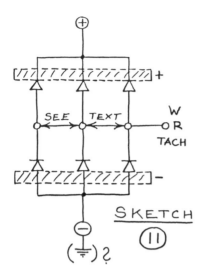

SEE TEXT

W
OR
TACH

SKETCH
(11)

$(\frac{1}{=})$ 2

show a short of stator windings to ground. Readings between 1 and 4 k Ohm may be due to the internal voltage regulator.

Other stator problems such as open windings are very unlikely unless the alternator had suffered severe damage. Tests of the individual three phase windings can only be carried out after disassembling the alternator.

Diode trio test

The diode trio consists of three small auxiliary diodes which separately rectify stator output, to supply field current. This separate plus output terminal is called D+, L, REG, "1", or EXC, or is referred to as light, charge light, or excite terminal. Failure of the diode trio causes the charge light to remain bright and prevents alternator output, due to lack of field current.

Test by bringing full 12 Volt to the diode trio terminal, by shorting the charge light terminals to each other (which will leave the charge light dark but bring 12 Volt from key switch to alternator), or by connecting a wire between plus 12 Volt and the diode trio terminal. If this returns alternator performance to normal, the diode trio is faulty. The wire may remain connected as an emergency repair. However, with engine off, the source of 12 Volt to the wire should also be switched off. Otherwise, about 3 Ampere will continue to be drawn and may drain the battery.

Alternator performance problems

Even though all elements of the alternator may be working in good order, there is a problem if the alternator is unable to fill its primary job on board, that of battery charging. We will look at several different cases, look for explanations, and discuss possible solutions.

SKETCH 12: shows battery or alternator output voltage from engine starting on, sketch is similar to **SKETCH 5**. Batteries are large, alternator is small or runs too slowly. Voltage never reaches the region above 14 Volt where most

voltage regulator settings are. The regulator keeps the alternator at maximum output throughout the plotted stretch of time, but alternator output current is so low that battery voltage rises only very slowly. To fully recharge batteries, running time would have to be very long.

Test: speed up engine and alternator while watching ammeter. A proportional increase in Amps with engine speed would be normal. Then a substantial increase in alternator speed, through an increase in engine pulley diameter, would be a good solution unless you could tolerate a higher speed of the engine itself.

SKETCH 13: Battery voltage rises normally, but levels out at a voltage below 14 V. The voltage regulator reduces alternator output too early, by maintaining this lower voltage, and batteries do not reach full charge.

Test: measure voltage directly at alternator output terminal after alternator has been running long enough to have battery voltage level out. If voltage is the same as battery voltage (allowing for wiring voltage drop of no more 2 tenths of a Volt), voltage regulator setting is too low. Since most regulators have no adjustment, use a diode of type 1N5400, connect in regulator sense wire, with band-marked end (cathode) toward regulator, opposite end toward battery plus.

If voltage at the alternator output terminal is 0.6 to 1.0 V higher than battery voltage while the alternator is running, you likely have charging diodes, also called isolating diodes, isolator, or splitter, wired as in **SKETCH 14**. The actual problem likely is the voltage regulator sense terminal which in many alternators is connected internally to the plus output terminal (anticipating that terminal to be connected directly to the car battery), or connected near the alternator to the output wiring, as in the sketch.

Reconnect as shown by the dashed line, to one of the two batteries. Best choose the one which is usually lowest in charge, such as a house battery rather than the engine battery. In this way, the voltage sensed by the regulator will be the actual battery voltage, not a voltage measured upstream of the voltage drop which occurs at the charging diodes. Or connect a type 1N5400 diode, band-marked end toward the regulator sense terminal, spliced into the sense wire.

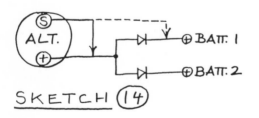

SKETCH (14)

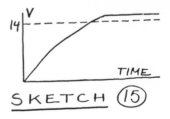

SKETCH (15)

SKETCH 15: after starting engine and alternator, the battery voltage rises nicely at appreciable rate, and to a level above 14 Volt, normal for most voltage regulators. The batteries are being charged fast, and to full recharge. In this case, the alternator is large and running at sufficiently high speed, but its capacity is only being used during the short time between engine starting and voltage reaching the regulator voltage setting. From that moment on, the voltage regulator begins to reduce alternator output, in order to maintain that voltage level.

In this case, it is important to connect all batteries on board to the alternator, to be charged at the same time. This presents the largest battery capacity or load to the alternator, so that the combined battery voltage will rise more slowly, keeping the alternator at maximum output longer and thereby generating more Ampere hours during a given length of engine running time.

Also in this case, installation of additional batteries, to increase total battery capacity, seems desirable.

Tachometer trouble

Tachometers sense engine speed by one of two methods. One of them uses the alternating current generated in the alternator. The tachometer "signal" is taken from one of the three stator terminals and is AC, before being rectified. Since the frequency is proportional to alternator speed which, in turn, is proportional to engine speed, this method works well most of the time.

Problem: tachometer reading goes up and down while engine, by ear, runs at steady speed. This is most likely caused by a slipping alternator belt. Verify by a simple test.

Test: with engine at steady fast idle speed (which with diesels is steady due to the governor), watch the tachometer needle while someone switches cabin lights, spreader lights, and other available electrical equipment on. If tachometer reading falls, and comes back to the original reading when all electrical gear has been switched off, the alternator belt has been slipping, allowing the tachometer to slow down.

Further confirmation: kill the engine and feel belt and pulleys on engine and alternator. They are probably hot. The cure is obvious.

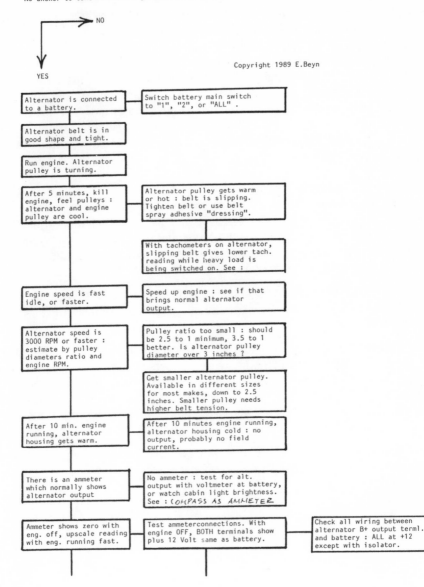

Alternator Troubleshooting Chart

YES answer to text in a box : go DOWN to next box.
NO answer to text in a box : go RIGHT to next box.

NO

YES

Copyright 1989 E.Beyn

Alternator is connected to a battery.	Switch battery main switch to "1", "2", or "ALL" .

Alternator belt is in good shape and tight.	

Run engine. Alternator pulley is turning.	

After 5 minutes, kill engine, feel pulleys : alternator and engine pulley are cool.	Alternator pulley gets warm or hot : belt is slipping. Tighten belt or use belt spray adhesive "dressing".

With tachometers on alternator, slipping belt gives lower tach. reading while heavy load is being switched on. See :

Engine speed is fast idle, or faster.	Speed up engine : see if that brings normal alternator output.

Alternator speed is 3000 RPM or faster : estimate by pulley diameters ratio and engine RPM.	Pulley ratio too small : should be 2.5 to 1 minimum, 3.5 to 1 better. Is alternator pulley diameter over 3 inches ?

Get smaller alternator pulley. Available in different sizes for most makes, down to 2.5 inches. Smaller pulley needs higher belt tension.

After 10 min. engine running, alternator housing gets warm.	After 10 minutes engine running, alternator housing cold : no output, probably no field current.

There is an ammeter which normally shows alternator output	No ammeter : test for alt. output with voltmeter at battery, or watch cabin light brightness. See : COMPASS AS AMMETER

Ammeter shows zero with eng. off, upscale reading with eng. running fast.	Test ammeterconnections. With engine OFF, BOTH terminals show plus 12 Volt same as battery.	Check all wiring between alternator B+ output terml. and battery : ALL at +12 except with isolator.

28

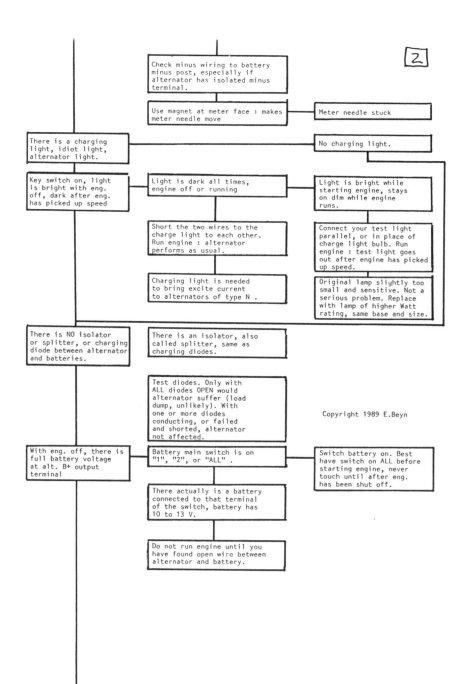

Check minus wiring to battery minus post, especially if alternator has isolated minus terminal.

Use magnet at meter face : makes meter needle move ——— Meter needle stuck

There is a charging light, idiot light, alternator light. ——————————— No charging light.

Key switch on, light is bright with eng. off, dark after eng. has picked up speed

Light is dark all times, engine off or running

Light is bright while starting engine, stays on dim while engine runs.

Short the two wires to the charge light to each other. Run engine : alternator performs as usual.

Connect your test light parallel, or in place of charge light bulb. Run engine : test light goes out after engine has picked up speed.

Charging light is needed to bring excite current to alternators of type N .

Original lamp slightly too small and sensitive. Not a serious problem. Replace with lamp of higher Watt rating, same base and size.

There is NO isolator or splitter, or charging diode between alternator and batteries.

There is an isolator, also called splitter, same as charging diodes.

Test diodes. Only with ALL diodes OPEN would alternator suffer (load dump, unlikely). With one or more diodes conducting, or failed and shorted, alternator not affected.

Copyright 1989 E.Beyn

With eng. off, there is full battery voltage at alt. B+ output terminal

Battery main switch is on "1", "2", or "ALL" .

Switch battery on. Best have switch on ALL before starting engine, never touch until after eng. has been shut off.

There actually is a battery connected to that terminal of the switch, battery has 10 to 13 V.

Do not run engine until you have found open wire between alternator and battery.

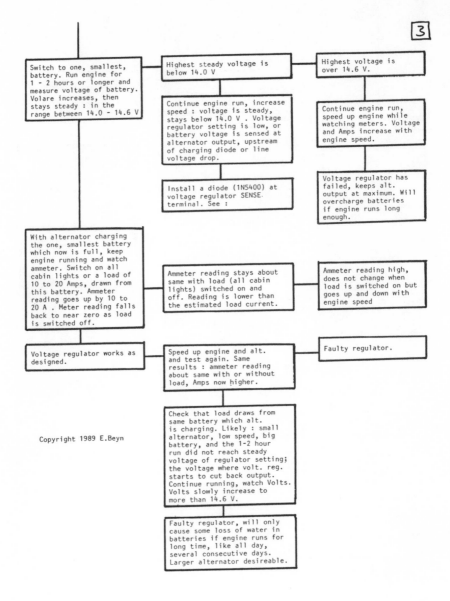

Switch to one, smallest, battery. Run engine for 1 - 2 hours or longer and measure voltage of battery. Volare increases, then stays steady : in the range between 14.0 - 14.6 V

Highest steady voltage is below 14.0 V

Highest voltage is over 14.6 V.

Continue engine run, increase speed : voltage is steady, stays below 14.0 V . Voltage regulator setting is low, or battery voltage is sensed at alternator output, upstream of charging diode or line voltage drop.

Continue engine run, speed up engine while watching meters. Voltage and Amps increase with engine speed.

Install a diode (1N5400) at voltage regulator SENSE terminal. See :

Voltage regulator has failed, keeps alt. output at maximum. Will overcharge batteries if engine runs long enough.

With alternator charging the one, smallest battery which now is full, keep engine running and watch ammeter. Switch on all cabin lights or a load of 10 to 20 Amps, drawn from this battery. Ammeter reading goes up by 10 to 20 A . Meter reading falls back to near zero as load is switched off.

Ammeter reading stays about same with load (all cabin lights) switched on and off. Reading is lower than the estimated load current.

Ammeter reading high, does not change when load is switched on but goes up and down with engine speed

Voltage regulator works as designed.

Speed up engine and alt. and test again. Same results : ammeter reading about same with or without load, Amps now higher.

Faulty regulator.

Check that load draws from same battery which alt. is charging. Likely : small alternator, low speed, big battery, and the 1-2 hour run did not reach steady voltage of regulator setting; the voltage where volt. reg. starts to cut back output. Continue running, watch Volts. Volts slowly increase to more than 14.6 V.

Faulty regulator, will only cause some loss of water in batteries if engine runs for long time, like all day, several consecutive days. Larger alternator desireable.

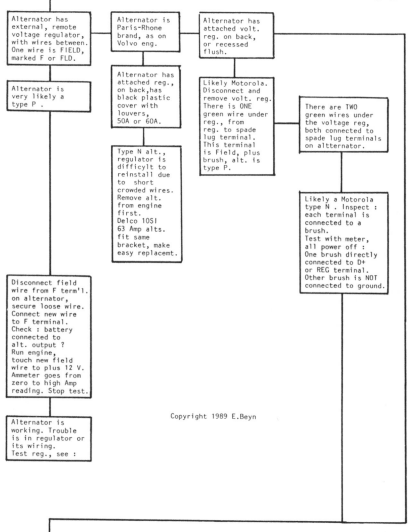

Alternator has
external, remote
voltage regulator,
with wires between.
One wire is FIELD,
marked F or FLD.

Alternator is
Paris-Rhone
brand, as on
Volvo eng.

Alternator has
attached volt.
reg. on back,
or recessed
flush.

Alternator is
very likely a
type P .

Alternator has
attached reg.,
on back,has
black plastic
cover with
louvers,
50A or 60A.

Likely Motorola.
Disconnect and
remove volt. reg.
There is ONE
green wire under
reg., from
reg. to spade
lug terminal.
This terminal
is Field, plus
brush, alt. is
type P.

There are TWO
green wires under
the voltage reg,
both connected to
spade lug terminals
on altternator.

Type N alt.,
regulator is
difficylt to
reinstall due
to short
crowded wires.
Remove alt.
from engine
first.
Delco 10SI
63 Amp alts.
fit same
bracket, make
easy replacemt.

Likely a Motorola
type N . Inspect :
each terminal is
connected to a
brush.
Test with meter,
all power off :
One brush directly
connected to D+
or REG terminal.
Other brush is NOT
connected to ground.

Disconnect field
wire from F term'l.
on alternator,
secure loose wire.
Connect new wire
to F terminal.
Check : battery
connected to
alt. output ?
Run engine,
touch new field
wire to plus 12 V.
Ammeter goes from
zero to high Amp
reading. Stop test.

Copyright 1989 E.Beyn

Alternator is
working. Trouble
is in regulator or
its wiring.
Test reg., see :

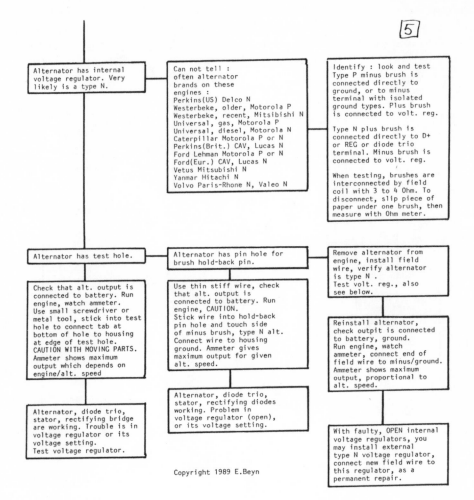

Alternator has internal voltage regulator. Very likely is a type N.

Can not tell :
often alternator
brands on these
engines :
Perkins(US) Delco N
Westerbeke, older, Motorola P
Westerbeke, recent, Mitsibishi N
Universal, gas, Motorola P
Universal, diesel, Motorola N
Caterpillar Motorola P or N
Perkins(Brit.) CAV, Lucas N
Ford Lehman Motorola P or N
Ford(Eur.) CAV, Lucas N
Vetus Mitsubishi N
Yanmar Hitachi N
Volvo Paris-Rhone N, Valeo N

Identify : look and test
Type P minus brush is connected directly to ground, or to minus terminal with isolated ground types. Plus brush is connected to volt. reg.

Type N plus brush is connected directly to D+ or REG or diode trio terminal. Minus brush is connected to volt. reg.

When testing, brushes are interconnected by field coil with 3 to 4 Ohm. To disconnect, slip piece of paper under one brush, then measure with Ohm meter.

Alternator has test hole.

Alternator has pin hole for brush hold-back pin.

Remove alternator from engine, install field wire, verify alternator is type N .
Test volt. reg., also see below.

Check that alt. output is connected to battery. Run engine, watch ammeter.
Use small screwdriver or metal tool, stick into test hole to connect tab at bottom of hole to housing at edge of test hole.
CAUTION WITH MOVING PARTS.
Ammeter shows maximum output which depends on engine/alt. speed

Use thin stiff wire, check that alt. output is connected to battery. Run engine, CAUTION.
Stick wire into hold-back pin hole and touch side of minus brush, type N alt.
Connect wire to housing ground. Ammeter gives maximum output for given alt. speed.

Reinstall alternator, check outpit is connected to battery, ground.
Run engine, watch ammeter, connect end of field wire to minus/ground.
Ammeter shows maximum output, proportional to alt. speed.

Alternator, diode trio, stator, rectifying diodes working. Problem in voltage regulator (open), or its voltage setting.

Alternator, diode trio, stator, rectifying bridge are working. Trouble is in voltage regulator or its voltage setting.
Test voltage regulator.

With faulty, OPEN internal voltage regulators, you may install external type N voltage regulator, connect new field wire to this regulator, as a permanent repair.

Alternator controls

Look at **SKETCH 4** in the alternator section, to see the two possible alternator designs, type N and type P. Always, the field coil and the voltage regulator are connected in series. But there are two possibilities which comes first: the regulator or the field coil. One works as well as the other, but type N regulators can only be used "downstream" of the field coil, on the Negative side, or spliced into the minus wire.

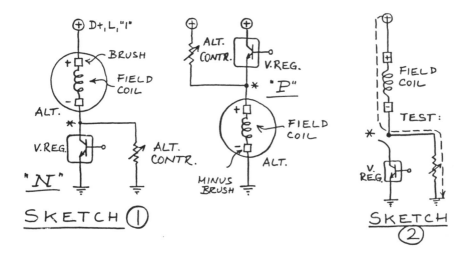

SKETCH 1 (in this section) shows the two designs again, here with a voltage regulator connected as well. The alternators do not show all of their terminals, only the field coil with plus and minus brush, and the voltage regulator. Most alternator controls work by allowing extra field current to flow, thus making the electromagnet, the rotor, more strongly magnetic. The alternator then produces greater output power at a given speed. The sketch shows that in each case, the alternator control, shown here simply as a variable resistor, is connected in parallel to the type N or type P regulator. The extra field current flows through the alternator control and thus bypasses the voltage regulator.

To test an alternator control, you may just wait long enough after starting the engine, to let the normal alternator output current fall to a low reading, then switch the control on, turn it up, and watch for an increase of alternator output.

Or you test the control by disconnecting the voltage regulator, as shown in **SKETCH 2**. A type N design is shown here, but the same test also applies to type P alternators. Disconnect the regulator at the *, secure the regulator wire. Then run the engine. With the control off, the alternator will have no output at all, and there will be no tachometer reading if the tachometer works with alternator signal. Then turn the alternator control on and up, to get output and ammeter readings.

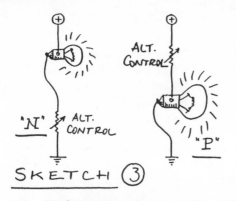

SKETCH (3)

A test of the alternator control by itself is shown in **SKETCH 3**, at left for a type N setup, at right for type P. The lamp which may be your test light, or a lamp with higher wattage up to the limit of the control, is taking the place of the alternator field coil. Turn the control up and down, to see the lamp go bright and dim.

The alternator control is shown here as a variable resistor. Early alternator controls were just that: rheostats with Ohm ratings between 10 and 20 Ohm, and with resistance wire sizes suitable to handle 3 to 4 Ampere. Electronic alternator controls such as the Spa Creek "AutoMAC", "T-MAC", or "AutoCHARGE", US Patent 4,687,983, use transistors to regulate field current. To test them, connect a test light as in **SKETCH 3** to take the place of the alternator field coil, then connect to plus and minus 12 Volt and see whether the light becomes bright gradually as the control is turned up.

Cabin lights

This part of the wiring consists mostly of switches and fixtures, and we might as well include most other electrical equipment below decks, such as fans, blowers, radios, tape players, which would all be similarly wired to battery power.

SKETCH 1 is bound to be similar to the wiring on your boat. The sketch starts with a battery plus post and shows one heavy wire (battery "cable") connected to the battery main switch. To help you identify the other, "common" or "feed" terminal of the battery switch, the heavy connection to the starter is shown. Otherwise, all other battery plus and minus wires are omitted to keep the sketch simple.

From the battery main switch, there is a modestly heavy wire of #18 or 10 to the "line" side of all circuit breakers. This wire is often called the feed wire, and it may come from the plus terminal of the starter solenoid instead of the battery switch. Electrically, that makes little difference: this wire comes from one or the other end of the starter "cable", obvious when you know where to look.

The common, line, or feed side of the circuit breakers or fuses also is easily recognized: all, or most of the terminals are interconnected, to each other, with a copper strap, solid heavy copper wire, or lots of short jumper wires. In the sketch, the top breaker controls the cabin lights. Your boat may have two breakers for separate circuits such as port and starboard, of forward and aft cabin lights, as the labels would tell.

The load side of the breaker in the sketch shows only a single wire: very unrealistic. More likely, that terminal will be the most crowded of all breaker terminals and may easily carry four or five wires, each connecting to a branch which could be as "a", "b", or "c" in the sketch. Treat each of these wires at the breaker separately, label each, and make your own sketch, or to verify any existing wiring diagram.

Trouble shooting between battery and the load terminal of the breaker is easily carried out with test light or voltmeter, connected across switches and possible (but unlikely) breaks in wires, as outlined in the beginning section. Also to be tested are all of the ground or minus wires which are not shown in the sketch. By convention, the plus part of the wiring carries all of the switches, and all minus wires are permanently connected. Before you test individual

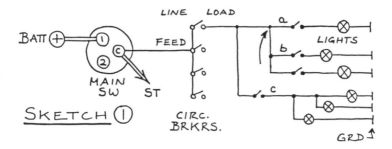

lights or groups of lights or branch circuits, test the connection to ground or to battery minus at a light which does not work. A long test wire or extension wire may be needed which you connect to battery minus or to engine ground and then touch to the minus terminal of a light which does not work. Minus wiring trouble would show itself if the light becomes bright.

Branch circuit "a" in **SKETCH 1** shows a single switch which powers a single light. Such switch is often mounted directly on the light fixture. The switch can be tested without disassembling the fixture if you can connect test light or Ohm meter (note: two different tests!) to the lamp socket terminals after removing the lamp. You would test across the switch to socket minus terminal with the test light and with power on, or across the switch with Ohm meter and power off. The lamp is tested easily with the Ohm meter, something you are surely familiar to you. Test the minus wiring if necessary.

Branch circuit "b" in **SKETCH 1** consists of two lights with their own switches, with the plus wire not on the circuit breaker but spliced to another plus wire. The location of the splice or joint may be difficult to find, but you would only have to look for it when all lights in that circuit fail and you find that the plus supply to at least one or two of the switches does not carry plus 12 Volt when the circuit breaker is turned on. In this case again, it is extremely unlikely that two or more switches fail at the same time, or that two or more lamps have burned out at the same time without an exterior cause such as a high voltage spike.

Branch circuit "c" in **SKETCH 1** is not very common but is trouble shooting relatively easy. A single switch controls several lights. If only one light fails, that lamp, its socket, and the plus and minus wires to that socket would require testing. Only if more than one light fail at the same time would their common wiring come under suspicion: the switch, the wires to and from the switch, and any common ground wire need to be tested. The plus wire to the switch at "c" likely starts at the circuit breaker and then does not start at some invisible splice as the sketch implies.

Wiring to tape players, stereo equipment, disk players often will have been added to existing wiring in the boat, and short cuts may have its wires connected to the cabin lights circuits at unusual places. Trouble shooting will mostly consist of tests of plus and minus wires at the equipment, and of your tracing the wires to the connections with existing wiring, and then of the usual tests at such joints.

Since the cabin lights wiring can be both complex and inaccessible, it is important to keep the symptoms in mind. If a single light fails while others work, the trouble is directly at that light or its individual switch or wiring, not at switches, wires, or circuit breaker which are in common use for other lights. On the other hand, if two lights fail at the same time, it is very unlikely that two lamps burned out at the same time. Here, suspect a switch or a wire which is used commonly by the lights which failed.

Engine Instruments and Alarms

Trouble shooting will be easy when you know how a particular instrument works. Temperatures and pressures are almost exclusively displayed with electrical meters, and the corresponding sensors are electrical. Only in rare cases will you still see a temperature gauge with capillary tube connected to a bulb in thermal contact with the engine. Such gauge though would be mechanical, and, except for its light, outside of electrical trouble shooting. The same applies to the rare pressure gauges which measure engine or transmission oil pressures with thin tubes, connected directly to the meters of the engine panel.

Temperature Instruments

The temperature sensing element called sender or sensor usually is a thermistor: a resistor which changes its resistance with temperature. The temperature gauge then is connected as in **SKETCH 1**. The engine key switch connects the meter to plus 12 Volt, and current through the meter is controlled by the thermistor TH. As it warms up, its resistance decreases and allows increasing current to flow. The meter is a milliampere meter with a temperature scale, matched to the thermistor.

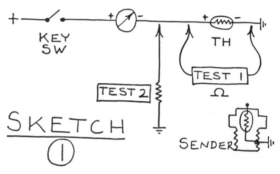

The circuit consists of the meter and thermistor in series. Electrically, it does not matter which comes first: plus, meter, thermistor, minus, or plus, thermistor, meter, minus. However, usually the temperature sender is built as in the small sketch, bottom, right, with one of its terminals connected to the threaded housing and to engine block ground. That way, the sender needs only one terminal and one wire. The other is the connection made by its threads. If your sender has just one terminal, your system matches **SKETCH 1**.

Tests of Temperature Gauge and Sender

The tests are shown in **SKETCH 1**. The sender can best be tested while on the engine. Use your VOM, switched to Ohm, as shown at **TEST 1**. Disconnect the wire from the sender. Measure with the engine cold, and find out if resistance decreases noticeably when the engine warms up. If it does, the sender is likely in good shape.

Use a resistor of about 100 Ohm, 2 Watt, or a small (!) test light and connect as **TEST 2**, from meter minus terminal to ground, or from the sender wire to ground. Touch briefly while someone else watches the meter, power switched on. The meter should give a reading, not related to temperature, telling us that the meter responds to current.

As additional test of the meter, measure the internal meter resistance, with power off, VOM switched to Ohm, meter test leads to the plus and minus meter terminals. Typical meters will have values between 100 and 1000 Ohm.

Since the whole circuit consists of just the meter and the thermistor, remaining trouble spots can only be the supply of plus power through the key switch or, on some engines, through more complicated paths including relays. There may be trouble in wiring between meter and sender, or at wire terminals, all easily checked: see the early chapters on basic trouble shooting techniques.

Pressure Instruments

Except for those rare mechanical pressure gauges which you recognize by the tubing, metal or plastic, connected on their back, engine pressure gauges are mostly electrical and, very similar to the temperature gauges described above, consist or a milliampere meter, in series with a sender. The sender changes electrical resistance as pressure changes, so that varied amounts of current flow through the meter. Performance is the same whether the circuit is plus-meter-sender-ground or in different order, plus-sender-meter-ground. Same as with temperature senders, it is simpler to wire the sender minus terminal directly to engine block ground: that is the arrangement shown in **SKETCH 2**. The sender, with the symbol for a variable resistor inside, is shown at the right in the sketch. Often, the pressure senders are relatively big, larger than, for example, pressure or temperature switches which you may find in similar locations on the engine. Electronic pressure sensors are available and are tiny in comparison but do not seem to have found their way into the engine instruments field.

Tests of Pressure Gauge and Sender

SKETCH 2 shows the tests: best check first that you are in fact dealing with an electrical system, keeping in mind that mechanical gauges may likely have lights, with the associated wiring.

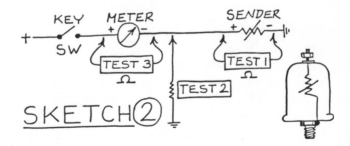

38

TEST 1

Test the sender: switch power off, use your VOM and its Ohm range, and connect to sender plus terminal which is the sole terminal on it. Connect the other meter lead to a clean ground spot on the engine block (which may require some searching!). Resistances other than extremely high or near zero likely show you a resistance element which is in tact.

To measure its resistance with pressure, see **SKETCH 3** and carry out the test near the engine instrument panel, rather than in the engine room. Disconnect the wire from the meter (or gauge) minus wire which is the wire to the sender. Use the Ohm range of the VOM and measure as shown. As you start the engine, you should see a significant change in resistance, usually from high to lower resistance. When killing the engine, resistance should change again, to about the original value.

TEST 2

As in **SKETCH 2**, connect a resistor between meter minus terminal and ground, or between sender terminal and ground, WITH POWER ON, engine off. The resistor should have about 100 Ohm, 2 Watt, or use a small (!) test light. Touch briefly while someone else watches the meter (gauge) which should give an upscale reading.

TEST 3

Another test for the meter: with power off, connect your VOM, Ohm range, to the meter terminals and measure the internal or coil resistance of the meter. Extreme readings, over 5 k Ohm, or zero Ohm, should make you suspicious. But other values, for example from 100 to 1000 Ohm, probably mean that the meter coil is all right. As long as the meter needle is not stuck, the meter, gauge, should be in working order.

Again, look at the wiring, terminals at meter and sender, and plus power source as possible trouble spots, keeping in mind that wires hardly ever just go bad, and that connections fail gradually.

Tachometer

There are three kinds of tachometers in use: one is mechanical, has a flexible thin drive shaft, may or may not have wires for a light, and is unimpressed with electrical trouble shooting techniques. The other two are electrical or, rather, electronic, and are shown in **SKETCH 4**. The back of their housing will likely tell which of the two you have.

Both of them likely have a light L, and both have plus and minus terminals for their supply of power. Both may have the light and plus power terminals

connected to the key
switch. They are different
because one has a single
S, Sender, Signal terminal
while the other has two.
The one on the left is connected to a terminal of the
alternator which sends alternating current to the
tachometer. The terminal
at the alternator may be
called R (Delco), A (Ford),
W (Bosch, Paris-Rhone),

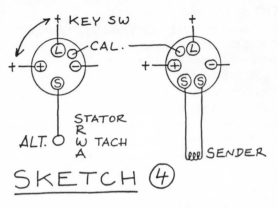

SKETCH ④

TACH (Motorola), or STATOR, which says what it is. The heavy stator windings in the alternator generate AC power which is the rectified, to become DC.
The frequency of the alternator current in the stator is strictly proportional to the
speed of the rotor in the alternator, and the tachometer electronics simply con-
vert frequency of the signal into a proportional voltage which moves the
needle.

Trouble shooting is limited to testing the proper input to the terminals of the
tachometer. Check plus and minus terminals with engine either on or off. With
the alternator type of tachometer, test the signal with your VOM turned to the
25 or 50 Volt AC range. Touch meter leads to the end of the signal wire, other
lead to ground, with engine running. You should see an AC voltage. If so, the
tachometer should be able to work with it, no matter how high or low your reading.

If there is no AC signal, make sure that the alternator is working by checking
ammeter or battery voltage rise, see the alternator trouble shooting section if
necessary.

Tachometers with a sender will often have that sender located on the engine
block, with the sender close to the teeth of the flywheel or some other geared
wheel. The sender can be a coil which generates pulses by induction when
steel flywheel teeth pass by, or may be a Hall sensor which is a solid state
component with its own amplifier, sensitive to magnetic changes when, again,
steel rear teeth pass close by. Trouble shooting is limited to checking connections. Only the inductive coil type sender could be tested for continuity with the
VOM, but the likelihood that such coil would develop a break in its windings, or
short the windings, is small.

Finally, there is an electrical tachometer design different from the ones in
SKETCH 4. This one does not use electronics but has a sensitive meter as its
display, connected to a small generator which is mounted on the engine and
driven by an extension of the cam shaft, or a special drive socket for that purpose.

SKETCH 5 shows one possible design. On the left, the generator most likely will have a permanent magnet on its rotor, and a stator coil to generate alternating current output. The meter on the right will be a sensitive voltmeter, connected through a rectifying diode and a dampening filter with resistor and capacitors. A calibration trim potentiometer is sketched near the meter. All of these components are likely in the meter housing.

The generator could be a DC type with brushes, built much like a DC permanent magnet motor, or the meter could be an AC voltmeter, with the AC generator shown in the sketch.

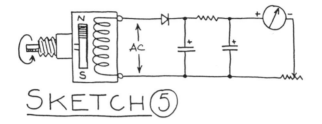

SKETCH ⑤

Testing the meter with your VOM switched to an Ohm range may easily produce a readout at the tachometer needle if the meter is in tact. Testing capacitors with the Ohm meter will give a large needle swing at first. The needle then must return to infinite Ohms, telling that there is no DC leak through the capacitor. And you are certainly familiar with testing the diode and resistors. In place of, or in addition the resistor, and inductance or coil could be used in the dampening filter here, but not likely since the frequencies from the generator are so low, even at high speed.

Testing the generator would consist of an initial check with the Ohm meter, to verify that its winding is in good order. From 200 to 2000 Ohm are probable readings. Then you may have to look for actual output: either test at the end of the wires from the generator-sender near the meter, or directly at the sender terminals, with engine running, if that can be done safely. As an alternative, you may be able to easily remove this sender from the engine. Be prepared to catch any drive keys or other small hardware. Then connect the VOM, switched to a low DC Volt or Milliamp range and spin the sender shaft. The meter should show pulses to plus and minus with each turn.

Batteries

Let us look at some battery problems and at some observations which you may view as problems but which may only need an explanation. Since very little can be done by you and me to repair a lead acid battery, the details here will relate mostly to battery treatment and mistreatment, and to maintenance.

Bad cells and hydrometer readings

Cells are usually declared bad when hydrometer readings of one cell remain low during charging, compared to other cells. The hydrometer measures electrolyte density, it distinguishes between heavier sulfuric acid in fully charged batteries and light electrolyte about like water, in discharged batteries. Charging releases sulfate ions from plates into the electrolyte so that it becomes heavier, and discharging the battery has sulfate ions go from electrolyte to the plates, to become part of the solids, leaving water.

As expected, the lighter solution tends to float to the top and the heavier tends to settle at the bottom. When recharging takes place while the battery sits essentially motionless, the hydrometer would sample the light layer on top of the plates, again and again, and detect little difference. Only with gassing, bubbles near completion of the recharge will agitate the electrolyte and bring more dense solution to the top.

Since there are bound to be small differences in both capacity and state of charge between the cells in a battery, the one cell with low density electrolyte may actually be the cell with biggest capacity, taking longer to begin gassing, and giving low hydrometer readings while other cells have reached full charge, have started to form gas bubbles, stirred the electrolyte, and produced higher density to the hydrometer in their top layer of solution.

Battery looses voltage after recharging

Immediately after charging, a new battery can reach as much as 13.8 Volt. With some age, or when made for use in the tropics, batteries can still reach over 13 Volt, but this reading then falls back by as much as 0.5 Volt within the first hour. This maximum of a completely charged battery can only be reached with some patience and relatively low charging current.

In practice, most recharging by alternator is carried out to a state less than complete recharge. When the engine and alternator are stopped, the batteries may show a voltage very close to the expected maximum, due to the outer surfaces of the plates being in fact completely recharged. Especially with deep cycle batteries and their thicker plates, active material deepest in the plates which had not been charged yet will share some of the energy from the outer surface of the same plate. As this equilibrium is slowly reached, battery voltage will fall. This effect is most noticeable when batteries are being recharged with high current, to levels of 50–70% of full charge. No Ampere hours are lost. But more could have been charged at a lower charging current.

Battery voltage

As a daily routine, and for sealed or badly accessible batteries, state of charge can better be measured by voltage than with the hydrometer. Important is to understand that battery voltage for this purpose must be measured while no current is flowing. With any charging or discharge current, the battery voltage will be higher or lower than the needed "standby" voltage.

SKETCH 1a shows battery voltage versus time, for a large battery while a very low current is being drawn. Interruption of this current will have no significant effect on the measured voltage. Note that the curve is near linear between about 20% and 80% of full charge. To make use of this gradual change of standby voltage, measure the highest voltage of your completely recharged batteries immediately after charging (range 13.0 to 13.8 V) and again about one hour after the end of recharging (in the neighborhood of 13 V), then discharge the battery with a lamp or resistor and measure voltage every half hour or hour. Interrupt the discharge current while measuring. Or use a percent meter with expanded scale, calibrated directly in percent of full charge.

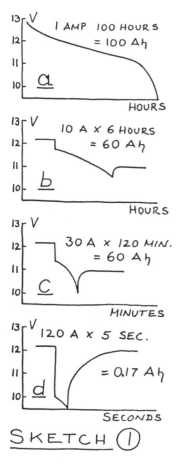

SKETCH 1

Battery capacity

The storage capacity in Ampere hours (Ah) is the significant measure of the size of a battery. The value is stated for new batteries but rarely measured. To determine battery Amp hours, start with a fully charged battery, connect a load, such as a number of cabin lights, and a voltmeter, and note the time. Total Watts of the lamps, divided by 12, give the average current in Ampere. Switch lights off when voltage has fallen to 11.0 Volt. Amps of the lights, times hours for the test give Ampere hours for the battery.

This test is important when you have to decide whether to replace a battery. Batteries with less than half of their original Ampere hours are candidates for replacement.

An Ampere hour tester is available which does the timing and switching automatically, so that you can let the test run its course and get the results at a later time.

SKETCHES 1b, 1c, and 1d show possible causes for errors or unnecessary concern over battery voltages. With a more substantial current of 10 Ampere drawn from a battery which, at the start, was charged at about 80% causes an instant drop in voltage, shown in SKETCH 1b. If the current is being drawn for

6 hours, 60 Ampere hours will have been taken from the battery. When the current is interrupted, battery voltage will recover, or increase to a value which corresponds to its state of charge.

This effect of voltage drop with current drawn, and voltage recovery after the current has stopped, is more pronounced with higher currents, or with the same current from smaller batteries, or a high ratio of current to battery capacity. In **SKETCH 1c**, 30 Amps are drawn from the same battery. Initial voltage drop, and gradual drop with the current are greater, and recovery after 120 minutes or 60 Ampere hours is greater, reaching the same standby value as in the previous example. In **SKETCH 1d**, starter current of 120 Ampere is drawn for 5 seconds, drawing a total of only 0.166 Ampere hours and having the battery standby voltage recover to about the value at the beginning. But the high current causes a sharp drop in voltage during that current. The more gradual voltage recovery is in hour, minute, and second scales but in reality is similar, and takes no more than a few minutes.

To understand the symptom, think of the battery as a sponge. Once completely soaked with water, one could touch dry paper towel to the sponge and withdraw water at slow rate, almost until all moisture has been taken out. But at a larger rate, it gets more difficult: even squeezing the water out of one end of the sponge would leave a lot at the other end which would only slowly travel to the drier end.

Cell voltage test

Quite some time ago, all batteries had their cells connected by lead bars on top of the battery: it was very easy to measure the voltage of each cell. With the connections inside, under the top surface of the battery case, the test of individual cells has become a little more difficult. The test is shown in **SKETCH 2**. As long as your batteries still have caps on the cells, even if the caps are part of one or two larger plastic lids, you measure by dipping two lengths of solder, lead-tin alloy, into the electrolyte of adjoining cells while the solder wires are connected to the voltmeter.

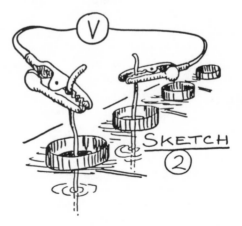

SKETCH 3 has the meter connected between battery minus post and the electrolyte in the lowest cell, test number 1. Test number 2 is between electrolytes in the lowest and the next cell, and so on, until the last test, number 7, between the electrolyte in the uppermost cell and the plus post. All readings should be about the same, around 2 Volt, and depending on the state of charge of the battery.

CAUTION: the electrolyte is dilute sulfuric acid, very dangerous to eyes, and corrosive to tools.

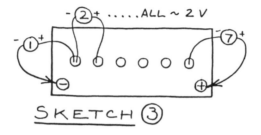

Nickel cadmium batteries

Cordless power tools, camcorders, rechargeable cordless shavers, and many other rechargeable electric gadgets use nickel cadmium or nicad batteries as their power storage. A single nicad cell delivers only 1.2 Volt, so usually several cells are connected in series, to supply a multiple of 1.2 Volt. The stainless steel cells are often packaged with plastic heat shrink tubing and may look as in **SKETCH 1**.

Although nickel cadmium batteries can last a very long time and can survive many years of storage, a single cell in the pack can fail suddenly, by becoming completely shorted on the inside. It then acts like a metal conductor. Charging and discharge current passes it, and the cell no longer contributes its 1.2 Volt to the total.

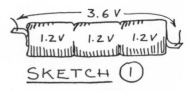

SKETCH ①

To test, charge the tool or the battery pack for the usual time, then use your voltmeter to measure the tool's battery, either at the outside socket for the charging connection, or inside, directly at the terminals of the battery pack. At that time, note and mark clearly the plus and minus terminals of the pack.

Normal voltage of a healthy battery pack is (number of cells) X 1.2 Volt. A shorted cell will have 3 cells give 2.4 V instead of 3.6 V, or 5 cells give 4.8 V instead of 6 V. The short develops when after many charging and discharging cycles cadmium metal has been electroplated to form a "tree" high enough to touch the opposite electrode and cause the short.

CAUTION: the method to cure shorted nickel cadmium battery cells can cause cells to explode. Proceed only after being fully prepared and protected, and after understanding what, and what not to do.

By very briefly applying high current to the battery pack, working cells will take on a charge and, within a few seconds, can develop excessive heat and burst their housing. High current for a very short time can melt or burn up the short in a shorted cell.

Make certain that the battery is in fact a rechargeable nicad battery. Do not try to charge or treat any alkaline or zinc-carbon batteries which may explode.

Use a small light or resistor to discharge the nicad battery pack, clip wires to the plus and minus terminals which you had clearly identified and marked. Then touch wires to posts of a 12 Volt battery as in **SKETCH 2**, for ONLY ONE SECOND. Disconnect and measure voltage. If the nicad battery is still 1.2 Volt low, touch to 12 V again for another one second. During this short time, the working cells in the pack will take on a charge and, with longer contact to 12 Volt, would heat and rupture their housings, spilling corrosive and strongly alkaline electrolyte. The electrolyte is the chemical opposite of acid.

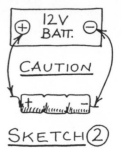

SKETCH ②

If several pulses of current are necessary, slowly discharge the battery pack again, let cool completely if it had warmed at all, repeat while keeping yourself protected, and keeping others out of the way.

Electrolytic Corrosion and Zincs

Different metals, isolated, by themselves, and under water, corrode at different rates: steel rusts fast, nickel corrodes hardly at all. When two different metals are in electrical contact with each other, and under water, an electric current is being generated as shown in **SKETCH 1**. While the less noble metal corrodes, electrons flow to the other, more noble metal, and ions travel in the water and complete the circuit.

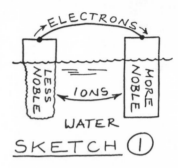

The current has an effect on each of the two metals: the less noble one corrodes faster than it would if isolated, and the more noble metal corrodes even more slowly than it would have by its own, isolated, not connected.

Dissimilar Metals in Water

Two examples of that effect are shown in **SKETCH 2**. At the top, a shaft zinc corrodes while sending electrons along the shaft and to the propeller. Ions again complete the circuit in the water, and the shaft and propeller are protected from corrosion due to the effect of the electrical current which is generated by the zinc.

At the bottom of **SKETCH 2** is a bronze screw, threaded into a piece of aluminum by mistake. The bronze screw is the more noble metal in this pair.

With water present, the aluminum corrodes at a rapid rate near the screw until aluminum hydroxide cuts down the current flow between the metals, by interfering with the electrical contact at the threads. At that time, the screw will likely come loose.

Corrosion from Electrical Current

SKETCH 3 has a battery connected to two pieces of metal which are in water. The metals may be the same or different. One metal corrodes because the battery causes a current which draws electrons from that metal. The water is any sea, river, or lake water, all of which contain enough dissolved salts to form the ions which complete the electrical circuit. Very few very noble metals can resist such electrolytic corrosion generated by an electric current. If the two metals were zinc and bronze, current from a 1.5 Volt battery, connected with minus pole to the zinc, would cause the bronze to corrode while keeping the zinc completely in tact. Stray current in the water is the second cause of electrolytic corrosion which we will investigate. Note the protective effect of electrons, with negative charge, in both **SKETCH 1** and **SKETCH 3**. Zinc generates these electrons in **SKETCH 1** while the battery does in **SKETCH 3**.

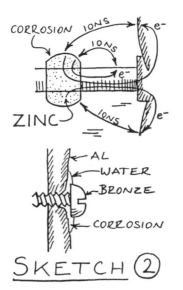

SKETCH ②

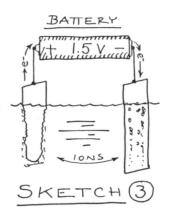

SKETCH ③

Metal Fittings on Fiberglass Hulls

We are looking at metal parts under water. Of these, some may be isolated, of corrosion resistant alloys such as true bronze, and not in need of corrosion trouble shooting. An example would be a bronze through hull fitting with rubber hose connected inside.

Greater attention would be due that same hull fitting if it were connected to a bonding or ground wire: the fitting then becomes a risk for stray current corrosion.

Our greatest attention belongs to metal assemblies made up from different metals, such as a stainless steel or Monel shaft with brass ("manganese bronze") propeller. In the water, the less noble metal would suffer as in **SKETCH 1**, unless a zinc "sacrificial anode" is also connected. The following tests should serve to prevent trouble, rather than correct.

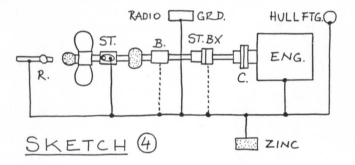

SKETCH 4 may appear complicated. There are two zincs, on the propeller and on the shaft. An additional zinc is shown connected to the bonding wire which interconnects hull fittings, radio ground plate, engine block with shaft and propeller, a strut, and rudder. The rudder would likely also have its own zinc. Stuffing box (ST.BX.) and stern bearing holder are likely isolated from the propeller shaft: the stuffing box by its packing and by the hose section used in its mounting, and the bearing holder fitting by the rubber cutless bearing. Separate bonding wires are shown as broken lines in the sketch. In practice, these wires are rare.

Another possible interruption of this circuit is at the coupling (C.), and possibly in the well lubricated bearings and gears in the gear box.

Hull-mounted zinc anodes are often installed as in **SKETCH 5**, with stainless steel hardware. The grounding or bonding wire is shown connected on the inside of the hull.

Testing While Hauled:

All tests look for electrical contact between zinc and metal fittings. Make up a long extension wire with clips, choose the lowest Ohm range of your VOM, and proceed as in **SKETCH 6**. Test directly from a cleaned, bright spot on each zinc to all metal parts below the waterline.

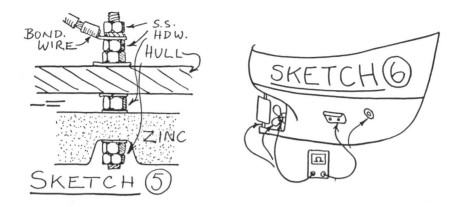

SKETCH 5

SKETCH 6

CAUTION: Meter performance

While digital Ohm meters can display small resistance differences, some Volt Ohm meters (VOM) can not. If necessary, make your own low-Ohm meter, or use a digital meter, to be able to detect connections which are in the 10 to 100 Ohm range, no immediate problem at that state, but potentially risky because resistance may increase with time, or with the boat back in the water.

Zinc on Individual Component

Rudders on sailboats and large rudders of wood or plastic often have a zinc mounted in a convenient place but some distance from the metal fitting which is to be protected. An electrical conductor is needed to connect the zinc to the fitting. Test as before, looking for electrical connection between zinc and fitting.

Zinc Mounted Directly on Metal Fitting

This is the zinc disk on metal rudders, propeller zinc, shaft zinc. Test from clean place on zinc, to clean place on the metal component, looking for near-zero Ohm readings as before.

In the Water Zinc Test

SKETCH 7 has the VOM switched to a 0–1 or 0–5 Volt DC range, with an extension wire connected to a piece of copper suspended over the side so that

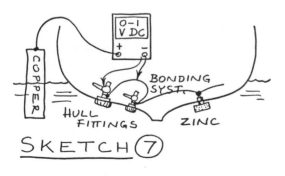

SKETCH 7

several square inches of only copper are in the water. For example, use a strip of sheet copper held by an alligator clip. Keep the clip out of the water. The boat here has a bonding system, with a zinc shown connected to two bronze through hull fittings. Touch the other meter wire to bonding wire, hull fittings, or bolt at the zinc. With a zinc in place and in working order, the meter should give a reading of greater than about 0.7 Volt. Without any zinc, the reading would be near zero.

With any trouble, first disconnect the bonding or ground wire at the zinc, then measure as in **SKETCH 7**, touching the meter lead to the zinc bolt. A reading of about 0.8 Volt should verify that there is a zinc on the outside of that bolt. Then reconnect the through hull fittings, engine block with propeller shaft, and any other fittings while you monitor the voltage measurement. You may find that there was a bad connection between zinc and its wire, or the zinc may turn out too small to impose its voltage on the hull fittings. Another zinc on a stainless steel wire, suspended over the side, and with the wire connected to the bonding, should prove the point.

Possible interference to this test may come from stray current. You may be able to correct for that by relocating your sheet copper electrode to the other side or end of the boat.

Stray Current Test

Purpose of this test is to detect voltage differences in the water between locations around your boat. Any such voltage will cause a stray current in the water. Your boat, with bonded fittings, may offer a more conductive path that the water, and stray current may then flow through your bonding system from one end of the boat to the other, or from side to side, or both.

SKETCH 8 shows how to connect two pieces of sheet copper to the VOM. Make the pieces 8 to 12 inches long and solder lead wires directly to the edges. Wires may be No. 16, 18, or thinner. Suspend the copper sheets on each side of the boat, and at bow and stern, and take readings on the 0–1 Volt range, both DC and AC, and with lower or more sensitive ranges if available. Exchange wires at the meter, to measure both DC polarities. Make a note of readings, together with the distance between the copper electrodes. Relocate the electrodes to find maximum volt-

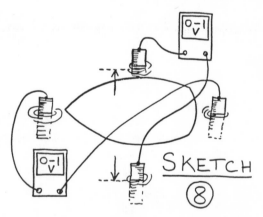

age which may be in a direction other than straight abeam or fore and aft. To increase sensitivity, disconnect bonding wires from fittings far forward, or disconnect wires which run from fittings port to starboard during the test.

With greater distance between electrodes you gain greater sensitivity. The result of this test is a voltage gradient, in Volt or Millivolt per foot: if you detect 0.1 Volt with electrodes 10 feet apart, the voltage gradient would be 0.01 Volt per foot, or 10 mV/FT. Obviously, two or more hull fittings, interconnected with bonding wire, will pick up voltage in the water just like the copper test electrodes. Since the meter's resistance is missing here, a current would flow from one fitting to the other, through the bonding wire. For one of the fittings, this current would reduce the protective current from the boat's zinc.

Once you have determined the approximate direction of any stray current, note its polarity, and select a bonded hull fitting in your boat which is farthest away from the plus copper electrode in your test, see **SKETCH 9**. "TEST RESULT" shows your earlier tests with polarity: the meter then had its plus wire at the electrode at the stern. A hull fitting forward in the boat is shown. Disconnect its bonding wire which connects to a zinc somewhere. Measure with the VOM lowest milliamp range:

> protective current from the boat's zinc(s) is still flowing, in spite of stray current around the boat, if the meter gives you a reading with plus lead on the hull fitting, minus on the disconnected bond wire. A current of just 1 milliamp will be quite sufficient for a through hull fitting of average size and alloy.

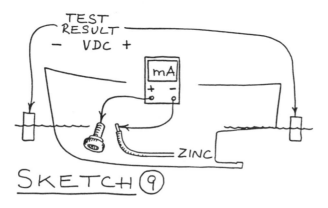

SKETCH ⑨

Shore Power Problems

In some marinas and at a few private docks, the most a serious corrosion trouble is related to the boat's connection to shore electric power on the dock. **SKETCH 1** shows two 110 Volt AC outlets, one on the dock, and one on the boat. Even though the plugs and sockets are usually different, you are probably familiar with these outlets: the two parallel slots supply the power, the additional half round socket is the ground connection. The slots are slightly different in length: the short one is hot, black wire, and the long one is neutral, white wire. The yellow shore power cable brings all three on board and to the other outlet in the sketch.

There is one additional connection in **SKETCH 1**: between the outlet ground terminal and the hull. This connection is made inadvertently, indirectly, by accident, sometimes on purpose. You can not simply disconnect it even though it is responsible for a great deal of electrolytic corrosion trouble on boats in marinas. But you can check easily if your boat is at risk. This connection, together with the ground wire in the shore power cable and the ground wiring on the dock, connects your boat's through hull fittings with those of many other boats nearby, and with all grounded electrical equipment on the dock and near shore.

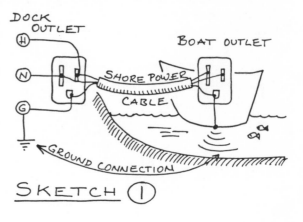

SKETCH ①

Ground Wire Tests

Purpose of the tests is to determine if shore power ground is connected to boat's ground and, if it is, whether any current flows in the shore power cable ground wire. Such current, electrons, will have an effect on the zincs and metal components under water.

Test: Boat's Ground to Shore Ground

Disconnect the shore power cable. Use the VOM, Ohm rang. Test the meter battery and adjust zero. Measure between the ground terminal of any (all ?) 110 V AC outlet and boat's ground, that is engine block, propeller shaft, grounded or bonded through hull fittings. Readings under 100 Ohm point to some metal-to-metal contact which may be unintentional or in poor condition. Readings between about 100 and 2000 Ohm may come through water in hoses, for example between a shore power grounded water heater and hoses to the engine. Higher readings may be difficult to explain, and would allow only very small currents between shore ground and boat's ground, with little effect. But repeat such measurements from time to time, to make sure they remain high.

Test: Current in Ground Wire

On purpose, there is NO SKETCH for this test. You have to read the text, in order to see the following

CAUTION: Do this test only if you fully understand the risk of touching the wrong, live, 110 Volt power terminal directly, or through a tool, or through the test wires of your Volt Ohm Meter (VOM). The measurement is **ONLY BE-TWEEN GROUND TERMINALS**. Make certain that you know which the ground terminals are, or have someone with the needed experience carry out the test.

CAUTION: You can be shocked through the Volt Ohm Meter. Do not touch one meter lead when the other may contact the wrong terminal of a 110 Volt outlet.

On board, disconnect the shore power cable and identify the two ground terminals. One on the cable is female. One on the boat's socket is male.

Switch the VOM to the 0–10 Volt DC range. Measure between shore ground and boat's ground by connecting one meter lead to the shore cable ground terminal slot which is often L shaped, touch the other meter lead to the corresponding lug of the shore power fitting on the boat. Keep in mind that the other end of the cable is plugged in, and two of the three slots at your end are dangerous.

With an Ohm reading in the first test, this test should give you at least a slight meter needle deflection or some low numbers on digital meters. If none at all, check all connections. With only slight needle movement or low numbers, switch to the next lower meter range until you get a clear indication of voltage and its polarity. Exchange meter leads if meter needle wants to pull below zero, or if the digital meter gives you minus values.

Note voltage and polarity: remember if boat is plus or shore ground is plus.

RESULTS: Look at **SKETCHES 1** and **3** in the previous section and note the direction of electron flow. If your measurement shows a voltage with the BOAT PLUS and SHORE GROUND MINUS, you are in luck because electrons will be poured on board when you reconnect the shore cable. However, if there is a voltage, with the BOAT MINUS and SHORE GROUND PLUS, electrons will flow from boat through the shore power ground wire to shore: electrons which were generated by your zincs, see the earlier section. Your zincs will be eaten up more rapidly and, when they become too small, the metal next in line will corrode, that is the one you wanted to protect most with the zinc.

Voltages up to about 100 millivolt will just speed the consumption of zinc, or help the zinc a little, depending on polarity, last paragraph. Voltages greater than 100 mV can become more serious, faster.

Test: Current in Ground Wire, Directly

With a voltage detected by the previous test, a current will flow in the ground wire, once the cable is reconnected between boat and dock. If your VOM is equipped with a milliampere range, you may try to measure the magnitude of the current through the shore power cable ground wire directly. With the meter first switched to the highest mA range, connect the meter as in the previous test. Read the CAUTION notes.

Zinc Consumption

For details about zinc protection see The 12 Volt Doctor's Practical Handbook. 100 milliamps will consume an additional ounce of zinc in about 10 days. Since a current between boat (minus) and shore (plus) will instantly diminish the protective effect of zincs on the hull, corrosion damage to propeller and hull fittings can occur long before the present zincs have been significantly reduced in size.

Corrective Action

You may NOT disconnect boat's ground from shore power ground unless you provide for personal safety from electric shock at the same time. Outlets on board must have ground terminals which are connected by ground wire to shore ground, in order to trip a circuit breaker when a short develops. Keep in mind that a current much greater than the circuit breaker Ampere rating must flow through the ground wire to trip that circuit breaker. Circuit breakers are fine to prevent electrical fires but of no use to prevent shock hazards. But help

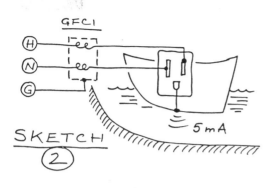

GFCI

SKETCH (2)

5 mA

is available in the form of ground fault interrupters, electronic devices which react fast enough to prevent shock hazards. You must test them regularly and, since they contain electronic components, must anticipate that they might fail and then not protect.

SKETCH 2 shows how they work, and how they are usually installed on the boat. Current in the hot and neutral wires is measured and compared. Without any loss or leak, exactly the same current must flow in both wires through the ground fault circuit interrupter (GFCI). This is the current which flows through the appliance. If there is a leak which allows some current to flow elsewhere, for example from hot or neutral wire, or from the windings of an appliance, to ground, that amount of current would be missed and make a mismatch in the GFCI. Leak currents greater than a few milliampere will trip the GFCI, compared with 25 or more Amps for a 20 Amp circuit breaker. As shown in **SKETCH 2**, current between boat's ground and shore ground through the water is then limited to about 5 mA. Note that the GFCI protects only the downstream wiring, not its own housing which must be grounded as usual. Typical installations have a GFC1-circuit breaker combination which takes the place of the shore power main breaker, on a panel or in a housing which is connected to shore power ground through the green wire in the shore power cable. However, boat's ground is then separated.

Test

Ground fault circuit interrupters have a test button and testing instructions. The test button connects a deliberate leak of borderline magnitude which must trip the GFCI.

A resistor of 25 to 30 kilo Ohm, ½ Watt, installed inside a plug, **SKETCH 3,** connected between one of the flat prongs and the ground prong, well insulated, can be used to test the GFCI from any outlet. But you must still go and reset. In cases of complicated wiring, such plug can help identify outlets which may not be connected through a GFCI.

Some less expensive VOMs may also trip the GFCI when measurements are taken between hot and ground terminals. The meter current then constitutes a leak to ground.

Finally, some reverse polarity alarms make use of the fact that full voltage exists between neutral and ground terminals when shore power has been connected reversed, hot and neutral switched. They will trip GFC1s if they draw enough power for their alarm.

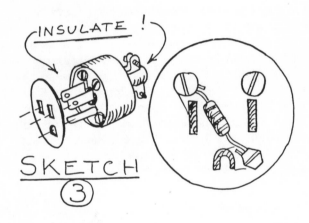

INSULATE !

SKETCH ③